Moving Singapore: From Rickshaws to Motorbikes

Raising a Singapore Family Business

BY EILEEN TAN @ EILEEN AUNG-THWIN

To order additional copies of this book, contact
Toll Free 800 101 2657 (Singapore)
Toll Free 1 800 81 7340 (Malaysia)
www.partridgepublishing.com/singapore
orders.singapore@partridgepublishing.com

ISBN
ISBN: 978-1-5437-5516-9 (sc)
ISBN: 978-1-5437-5518-3 (hc)
ISBN: 978-1-5437-5517-6 (e)

Library of Congress Control Number: 2019917249

Print information available on the last page.

10/30/2019

PARTRIDGE

"Work is love made visible."
- Kahlil Gibran

To Dad

Contents

Now, when I see a SingPost delivery bike or Traffic Police bike, I see an entire fleet and the support system behind it. *Moving Singapore: From Rickshaws to Motorbikes* is a short but fascinating read about the man who, out of the ashes of his motorbike retail shop in Beach Road, built a company that has become a leading player in the industry – supplying, maintaining and repairing thousands of two-wheelers in the delivery, transport and security sectors.

Robert Tan, chairman of Ban Hock Hin, is in a league of his own. He did not have much of an academic background to boast about. But what he had was a quick and sharp mind that helped him not only grasp the details but also see the big picture as well as the way ahead. He was able to know a good thing when he saw one even though he may not have fully understood the "how's" behind it. He had the courage to go out of his comfort zone and to take risks that others baulked at. And he possessed an understanding of what customers needed and how people behaved. You could say he is an entrepreneur, visionary and behavioral psychologist all rolled into one. Coupled with his sense of integrity, filial responsibility and humility, he is a businessman with a big heart.

Singapore could do with many more Robert Tans.

> *- By Judith d'Silva, retired civil servant and former member of the Speak Good English Movement*

Moving Singapore is at its core a remarkable story of a man who, within a single generation, beat the odds and built a thriving, innovative business in two-wheelers, based on the simple, yet powerful principle that working people in Singapore needed an affordable form of private transport. While in part a family history of the motorcycle industry, *Moving Singapore* is also a tale of the Henghua community, a sub-group within the broader Hokkien diaspora who played a crucial role in the development of Singapore's transport infrastructure. In doing so, the book draws reader's attention to the city-state's longer settler history and the contributions that the "Pioneer" and "Merdeka" generations made towards the country's development. *Moving Singapore* relates a story of nation-building from below, a glimpse into how an extraordinary man's quest to connect common people via affordable, individualized transport contributed to the broader integration of Singapore.

> *- Maitrii Aung-Thwin, National University of Singapore*

From the author

The idea for this book was planted more than a decade ago when a historian became fascinated by the story of Ban Hock Hin and of my father and encouraged me to write that story down. I finally had the chance to act on the suggestion in the year that both my father and Ban Hock Hin turned 80.

My father, Robert, was the source of much of the information captured in the following pages. His siblings – Bee Bee, Chin Bee and Richard – also contributed a great deal of information, especially those about the family's history. Other family members like my cousin Su En (Denyse) and my mother, Alice, also shared their recollections and photos. I can't thank them enough for helping me make this book happen.

Where possible, I've used scholarship and newspapers to provide some context, to double-check facts, or to corroborate accounts. Some of the information I was not able to verify. This book, therefore, is a collection of memories and perspectives as we know or remember them – not necessarily facts.

I'd like to thank my family and friends who read the drafts, shared their suggestions, and kept me going with their encouragement and support (Su En, I'm looking at you!). Much thanks to my friend Judith who proofread the manuscript in record time and helped me clean and polish the copy. I am also grateful to her for pushing me to write better and more clearly.

Special mention goes to Maitrii, my husband, without whom this project would likely not have been conceived and certainly not completed. His unstinting generosity, support, and optimism were vital to this book. Thank you, my love.

1890s to 1940s: Kow Sai and San Chwee

Rickshaw Roots

Robert stood in front of the burnt husk of a building that once housed his family's business and childhood home. In just a few pre-dawn hours, the flames had consumed 40 years' worth of toil. A sodden, soot-blackened facade stood where the front of the shophouse should've been. Instead of shiny Japanese-made motorcycles, melted rubber and twisted metal now littered the shop floor. Robert had received a phone call in the early hours of the morning telling him that the business he'd taken over from his father only a decade ago was burning down. By the time he'd rushed to 131 Beach Road from his home in Toh Tuck Place, all he could do was pick through its remains.

Robert Tan, born Tan Bee Chuan, is the eldest son of Tan San Chwee (陈山水 or *Chen Shan Shui* in Mandarin, meaning 'water from a mountain'). San Chwee was the middle son of a rickshaw puller turned shipbreaking businessman, Tan Kow Sai. Although born Tan Shen Heung (陈善馨 or *Chen Shan Xin* in Mandarin, meaning 'pervading virtuousness'), he was known as Kow Sai – or Dog Shit – his whole life. To many Chinese, a good name was vitally important to the life and fate of a person. Some believed that a name that complemented the person could elevate his lot in life, whereas a name that was unsuitable – sometimes, even one too grand for his constitution – could pin him down. And some believed that a crude – even vulgar – nickname could shield a beloved child from the attention of malevolent spirits out to create even more misery in a time of hardship and high infant mortality. The cruder and more vulgar the nickname, the greater the protection, and the deeper the parents' affection. Kow Sai's parents must have loved him very much.

Kow Sai was born in a village called Dong Ao (东澳 or *Dang Oh* in Henghua) in Pingtan, a municipal county of Fuzhou, the capital of Fujian province. The tiny fishing village is located at the eastern tip of China closest to Taiwan. Although the villagers identify as Henghua, the village is administered under Fuzhou, also known as Hockchew. The Henghua were originally from central China but migrated to present-day Putian in Fujian province[1]. The Henghua language is quite distinct and unintelligible to those in southern Fujian, who speak Hokkien.

---

[1] https://www.straitstimes.com/singapore/at-a-loss-for-words-try-henghua

Kow Sai fled the crushing poverty and social chaos that was an ailing China in the late 1800s, one of the millions that left Fujian and Kwangtung province between 1880 and 1940[2]. After surviving the arduous journey by ship to arrive in Singapore, like many other Henghua, he entered the transport trade and became a rickshaw puller. The rickshaw was a Japanese invention[3] called *jinrickshaw* or rikishas. It was introduced in Singapore in 1880[4], roughly around the same time the first Henghua arrived in Singapore[5]. By the time the Henghua arrived, other dialect groups such as the Hokkien were already well established in various trades and occupations[6].

The Singapore Chinese were organised in various dialect groups, and each group formed a *bang*, or a social grouping which took the form of associations, clans or guilds. *Bang* members enjoyed protection and support with the basic necessities of life, such as food, shelter and jobs. Earlier migrants to Singapore chose occupations according to their dialect groups because it was easier to work with people who spoke the same language and came from the same clan. In some cases, businessmen who needed more labour would write home to their clansmen in China for more men. Often, apprentices and workers would eventually leave their masters or employers and set up their own businesses in the trade they had learned, thereby expanding the industry. And in so doing, some trades came to be dominated, if not monopolised, by certain dialect groups. For example, the Hakka came to dominate the Chinese Medicine and pawn broking businesses[7]. The Hokkien were masters of trade, banking, finance, insurance and shipping[8]. The Hainanese cornered the coffee shop industry, and the Cantonese, the entertainment industry[9].

It was difficult for Chinese of different dialects to enter a trade already held by another. Thus, the newly introduced rickshaw industry gave the Henghua *sinkeh* (or 'new guest') an opportunity for trade and livelihood. They were also willing to work for less than their Hokkien and Cantonese peers who had entered the rickshaw pulling trade before them[10]. Dominance in the rickshaw trade also paved the way for the Henghuas to eventually dominate the transport trade as they later expanded into the trishaw, bicycle, motorcycle, taxi and automobile spare parts industries[11].

[2]   James Francis Warren, *Rickshaw Coolie: A People's History of Singapore 1880 – 1940*, Singapore: Singapore University Press, 2003, p. 15

[3]   Singapore Infopedia: http://eresources.nlb.gov.sg/infopedia/articles/SIP_947_2005-01-25.html

[4]   Singapore Infopedia: http://eresources.nlb.gov.sg/infopedia/articles/SIP_947_2005-01-25.html

[5]   Jason Lim, *A Slow Ride Into The Past: The Chinese Trishaw Industry in Singapore, 1942-1983*, Clayton: Monash University Publishing, 2013, p. 40

[6]   Ibid, p. 39

[7]   Singapore   Infopedia: http://eresources.nlb.gov.sg/infopedia/articles/SIP_1497_2009-04-09.html?s=chinese%20dialects%20in%20singapore

[8]   Singapore   Infopedia: http://eresources.nlb.gov.sg/infopedia/articles/SIP_1498_2009-04-09.html?s=Hokkien%20community

[9]   Interview with Robert Tan

[10]   James Francis Warren, *Rickshaw Coolie: A People's History of Singapore 1880 – 1940*, Singapore: Singapore University Press, 2003, p. 15

[11]   Jason Lim, *A Slow Ride Into The Past: The Chinese Trishaw Industry in Singapore, 1942-1983*, Clayton: Monash University Publishing, 2013, p. 41

According to historian James Francis Warren, the rickshaw 'revolutionized the life of Singapore'[12]. It changed the way Singapore residents moved about the city – Singapore traffic was largely pedestrian before rickshaws provided a form of cheap mass transport[13]. Within a year of its introduction, some 1,000 rickshaws plied the streets for hire and quickly replaced the horse-drawn gharry as the mass transportation of choice[14].

But rickshaw pulling was no easy trade. The other dialect groups thought it demeaning[15]. The work was extremely strenuous and the conditions, harsh and dangerous. Men have been known to fall over dead from over-exertion[16]. Motorised vehicles posed a deadly threat, especially from 1914 and on, after motor cars were introduced[17]. Disease and death were also rampant because of coolies' squalid living conditions. An article in *The Straits Times* quoted the Attorney General calling rickshaw pulling "the deadliest occupation in the East (and) the most degrading for human beings to pursue".[18] The work was considered so hazardous the colonial government abolished double-seated jinrikishas in 1912 on 'humanitarian grounds'.[19]

Eileen Tan @ Eileen Aung-Thwin

---

[12]   James Francis Warren, *Rickshaw Coolie: A People's History of Singapore 1880 – 1940*, Singapore: Singapore University Press, 2003, p. xiii

[13]   Ibid, p. 51

[14]   Ibid, p. 14

[15]   Jason Lim, *A Slow Ride Into The Past: The Chinese Trishaw Industry in Singapore, 1942-1983*, Clayton: Monash University Publishing, 2013, p. 40

[16]   James Francis Warren, *Rickshaw Coolie: A People's History of Singapore 1880 – 1940*, Singapore: Singapore University Press, 2003, p. 142

[17]   Ibid, p. 282

[18]   Double Rikishas (1912, Oct 28). *The Straits Times*, p.8. Retrieved from NewspaperSG

[19]   Ibid

4

A bronze sculpture of a rickshaw puller and his wealthy Peranakan passenger by award-winning Singaporean sculptor Lim Leong Seng. The sculpture sits in China Square Central in the Chinatown area. Bronze seems an apt medium – rickshaw pullers' lives were desperately hard, and the men needed to be even harder to survive the occupation.

Unlike many of his brethren, Kow Sai didn't stay in the rickshaw trade. Family lore has it that while pulling rickshaws, Kow Sai came to ferry a British official quite regularly, likely under monthly contract, which was common then. The unnamed British official took a liking to Kow Sai, and when the official planned to leave Singapore, it seemed he gave Kow Sai a licence to break or recycle ships. Apparently, it was one of only three available licences at the time. Although hard and dangerous work, it was a lucrative trade. To cash in on this windfall, Kow Sai had to acquire a ship to recycle. However, when he went to the shipyard looking to buy a ship, he was met with derisive laughter and incredulity that a dirt-poor rickshaw puller would want to buy a ship. Someone told him in jest that he'd sell a ship to him for $50 – if Kow Sai *had* $50. Kow Sai returned to the British official with his tale, and his benefactor handed over the $50, setting Kow Sai on his path to his new career – and fortune.

Details about how Kow Sai went on to build his riches are scarce. By the time I started collecting family stories, there were no more relatives of his generation or the next to ask. Robert speculates that Kow Sai probably turned to his *bang* for labour and other resources to build his shipbreaking business. All family members know is that Kow Sai became quite wealthy and had three sons and three daughters.

Tan Shen Heung (1879 – 1934), or Kow Sai, who came to Singapore as a rickshaw coolie and made his fortune in shipbreaking. This is the photo on his tombstone in Bukit Brown cemetery.

But wealth was not to remain in the family. After Kow Sai died in 1934 at the age of 55, the family lost its fortune. It seems Kow Sai's eldest son, Boon Hong, was a gambler, and much of the family coffers was used to feed his gambling habit. But the financial death knell was rung when Boon Hong was caught in a grave indiscretion. In exchange for his life and freedom, his mother had to fork over the bulk of the family's remaining wealth, thus bringing the family to its financial knees.

San Chwee, Robert's father, was reportedly very resentful of his eldest brother for ruining the family's and his own prospects. In 1936, San Chwee's mother arranged for the 16-year-old boy to marry the youngest daughter of a wealthy Qing Dynasty magistrate who had migrated to Singapore from Amoy or Xiamen in southern Fujian province. She was also 16.

The Qing magistrate was surnamed Chionh, the same surname as Chiang Kai Shek, the military leader of Taiwan under the Kuomintang, only spelt differently. Family members have little information about him and only know that he was high ranking – he wore a beautiful white jade ring on his thumb. Once used in archery by fearsome Manchu warriors, the thumb ring eventually evolved into a symbol of status and wealth in Qing China. Magistrate Chionh's ring was made of precious Burmese jade.

Ancestor Chionh's jade ring denoting his high status in Qing society.

When the elderly magistrate came to Singapore, he took a beautiful young Peranakan wife, or 'huan bor' meaning 'Malay wife', and Chionh Kim Lian was their youngest of six children, three boys and three girls. By family members' accounts, the elderly man adored his young wife, Tan Beng Tee, and spoiled her through and through. He also doted on his youngest daughter.

However, Kim Lian's young life came to be more a bed of thorns than roses. At her birth, a soothsayer divined that she was a *ke xin* or 'cursed star' upon her father's life. If she stayed in the household, her father would die when she was in her ninth year. Alarmed by the ominous prediction, Kim Lian's mother wanted to give the girl away but the old man wouldn't hear of it. He died nine years later.

Kim Lian's mother blamed her for the death of the elderly patriarch and tried to expel her from the household, fearing that her presence would bring more disaster upon the family. But no matter how many times Kim Lian was given away to other families, the little girl would escape and find her way home. After seven attempts at booting Kim Lian from the Chionh household, her mother finally gave up trying. Little did she know then that her 'cursed star' would one day be the family's *jiu xin* or saviour.

When Kim Lian reached a marriageable age, her mother had high hopes that she would be hitched to a wealthy family. Although the Chionh family's own fortunes had waned with the passing of its patriarch, to unwitting outsiders it was still a family of considerable stature and influence. At one time, the Chionhs apparently owned rows of shophouses. Thus, their daughters and sons were still seen as desirable assets to prospective in-laws, who would themselves, naturally, be equally influential and affluent. After all, she had already successfully matched her eldest daughter to an extremely wealthy Peranakan man. That wedding celebration had run on for days, and the prized match had been paraded in the streets with much fanfare.

Hence, when a matchmaker proposed a marriage with the middle son of a shipbreaking businessman, Kim Lian's mother was quite pleased. San Chwee's mother, too, likely thought that a match with a family of such an illustrious background as the Chionhs would help San Chwee's star rise. But this was a badly miscalculated move.

Once the true natures of both families' financial situations were revealed after the marriage, Kim Lian's dowager of a mother was enraged. Lore has it that she sought 'justice' from her *bang* for what she considered the matchmaker's deceit. We were never told what form justice took.

The two young teens San Chwee and Kim Lian carried on with married life, as nothing else could be done, and soon, two daughters – Cheng Jin and Cheng Bee – were born in quick succession. Marital life wasn't entirely peaceful, however. San Chwee's mother-in-law, whom the children came to call Nyonya Ma, showed little restraint in concealing her disappointment in the match. Much of her rancour was directed at San Chwee's impoverished status. One of San Chwee's daughters would later recall hearing about how her maternal grandmother would say of her dad: "*Bo lui ah ai chuay bor*" essentially meaning that San Chwee had no business getting married since he was a pauper. Thus, in 1939, San Chwee's mother gave him $150 – possibly his entire inheritance – to set up his own business and, hopefully, to make his own fortune.

One hundred and fifty dollars was not a princely sum, even back in 1939, not as far as business capital went. But $150, shrewd business acumen, and a burning desire to show up his detractors would prove a potent combination. Given his Henghua background, the 19-year-old San Chwee looked to the transport trade which many of his clansmen plied.

Singapore's transport scene in 1939 was a lively and chaotic one. Bicycles, rickshaws, motorcars and even a handful of handcarts and bullock carts jockeyed for space on the crowded roads. The most common vehicle then was the bicycle. With a starting price of $10[20] compared to $475 for a used Triumph motorcycle[21], the bicycle was the working man's choice of transport.

Some 93,000 bicycles and 7,000 tricycles plied the roads of Singapore in 1939[22]. The bicycle trade was already the domain of the Henghua, thanks to a Henghua called Yeow Kee[23] who was recorded as the first Chinese to venture into the bicycle trade. His company in Kuala Lumpur, the Hock Leong Hin Bicycle Company, became the training ground for many other Henghua who eventually left the company and migrated to other parts of Malaya and Indonesia to set up their own bicycle shops.

The number of Henghuas involved in the bicycle trade started increasing from the turn of the century, and by the time San Chwee was contemplating his future, the Henghua already dominated the field in Singapore. Thus, it would have been natural for San Chwee to start a bicycle business given the two-wheeler's popularity and his dialect connections. But given his limited capital, he could begin only with repairing the machines. He rented a space in a shophouse at Cross Street and started his business with one assistant, fixing up bicycles on the five-foot way. He named his business Ban Hock Hin, meaning 'to prosper with a thousand blessings'.

As fate would have it, on 12 November that same year, 19-year-old San Chwee celebrated the arrival of his firstborn son, Tan Bee Chuan (meaning 'perfect in wholeness'), who would come to inherit and define much of the business that San Chwee started.

---

[20] Registering Bicycles (1939, Jan 6), *Morning Tribune*, p. 10. Retrieved from NewspaperSG

[21] *The Straits Times*, Advertisements, Column 2 (1940, April 2), p. 1. Retrieved from NewspaperSG

[22] Island's Road Fatalities Down 58 per cent (1940, April 7), *The Straits Times*, p. 9. Retrieved from NewspaperSG

[23] Nanyang Daxue Lishi Xi 1971:34-35, as cited in Jason Lim, 2013, p. 41

The young couple with their first three children. From left to right: Cheng Jin, San Chwee, Bee Chuan (Robert), Kim Lian, and Cheng Bee. Circa 1940 - 1941.

The early years of Ban Hock Hin were hard and humble. San Chwee and his assistant repaired bicycle inner tubes; Kim Lian continued to bear him children. Two boys born after Bee Chuan failed to survive infancy.

In February 1942, the Japanese marched into Singapore, seized it from the British, and renamed the island Syonan-To, or "Light of the South Island". The Japanese thought themselves liberators of Asia from European influences. But in Singapore, they singled out the Chinese community for terror, torture and death because of the support of the overseas Chinese for China in the Sino-Japanese War. The Tans and their relatives were not unscathed. Nyonya Ma's eldest and second sons were rounded up by the Japanese along with thousands of other Chinese men, driven to an isolated part of the island, forced to dig their own graves, and were then mowed down by bullets. Miraculously, the eldest son survived but his mind did not. Robert and his siblings remember their 'Tua Koo' sitting wordlessly in a corner, staring unseeingly into the distance.

Robert, who was three when the Japanese Occupation started, has vague memories of Japanese soldiers wearing long swords entering San Chwee's shop. It seemed like they were searching for something, but they eventually left without incident. He also remembers watching a fight break out in the warehouse across from Ban Hock Hin. Japanese soldiers came, made the bare-bodied men line up, and took them away.

Misery was not the only thing the Japanese brought with them, however; for some, they also brought opportunity. In occupied Singapore, petrol was scarce. Leg-powered forms of transport – such as bicycles and trishaws – were therefore popular. This was good news for those in the bicycle trade. The Japanese tended to leave businesses and businessmen alone, as they needed to keep the economy functioning. Thus, San Chwee's bicycle repair business picked up, and he could operate in relative peace. Having got a little more money and needing more space, the family and business moved to a shophouse at 131 Beach Road, which they rented from an Arab landlord. San Chwee conducted his bicycle business on the ground floor while the family lived upstairs.

One of San Chwee's daughters[24] remembers her mother telling a story of how one day, while she was in the family living space above the shop with a babe in arms, a Japanese soldier came up the stairs. Initially startled and fearful, Kim Lian was both surprised and bemused when the soldier started smiling and chattering away at her. He seemed delighted to see the baby. He pulled out a photo of a woman and a baby, presumably his wife and child, to show Kim Lian and chattered away at her for a little while more. The soldier would visit several more times, each time bringing her some condensed milk.

But for a lot of others in Singapore, the Japanese Occupation was a desperate time. Hunger drove people to find all kinds of ways to survive. Some women would sell their bodies to feed their families, and some families would sell their children to create better opportunities for either the sellers or the sold.

It was during these desperate times that the Tan household gained a new member. It seems Kim Lian hated the drudgery of domestic life and its endless cycle of childbearing, child rearing, cooking and cleaning. Kim Lian's eldest sister then suggested Kim Lian take a servant girl as a second wife for San Chwee to help shoulder the domestic burdens. Both the circumstances and the polygamy norms of the time meant that it was not unthinkable for girls to be taken into a better-to-do household as both junior wife or concubine and servant. For some of those involved, it was likely a better option than many alternatives.

Koh Ah Choo, the woman the family came to know as Ah Yee, was brought into the Tan family sometime during the Japanese Occupation. Ah Yee gave San Chwee a son, born Tan Cheng Chuan but later known as Harry, in 1943. The industrious Ah Yee became the caregiver – and to many of the children, the pillar – of the household. Ah Yee cooked, cleaned and cared for the family, including the rest of Kim Lian's children who came after – Bee Bee, Siew Bee (Rosey), Chin Bee (Diane) and Kah Chuan (Richard).

---

24   Bee Bee

San Chwee and five of his children. From left to right: Bee Chuan (Robert), Cheng Jin, Bee Bee, San Chwee, Cheng Bee, and Cheng Chuan (Harry). Circa 1945 or 1946.

When the Japanese Occupation came to a seemingly abrupt end in 1945, many became paupers overnight when the 'banana money' – or the Japanese-issued currency they forced the population to use – became instantly worthless. Bee Bee remembers hearing stories of a greatly peeved Nyonya Ma burning banana notes and soundly cursing the Japanese.

San Chwee's war-time savings were spared the flames, however. Before the Japanese Occupation ended, he was tipped off by a Japanese soldier he was friendly with that things were going badly for the occupiers. Perhaps it was the same soldier who brought Kim Lian the condensed milk. Robert thinks now that his father had bought numerous goods with his banana notes while they were still accepted – products that he could sell for the next currency. Robert remembers the house and shop filled to the brim with random items. It would appear that San Chwee never passed the Japanese soldier's tip on to his mother-in-law.

From Two Wheels to Three

After the war, San Chwee's star began to rise. Although Singapore at large faced huge economic problems, such as high unemployment and slow economic growth, San Chwee's business picked up as he traded in a relatively cheap but essential product – the bicycle. Sometime during the war, he finally had enough capital to start selling, not just repairing, the machines. Across the street from his home and business was Beach Road market, also known as Clyde Terrace Market, which was the biggest market selling uncooked food in Singapore[25]. From his vantage point, San Chwee had plenty of time to observe the goings-on at the market, and he saw how the traders struggled with moving the bulky goods using wooden carts. And so, he came up with the idea that would propel him to his first big business success: the carriage tricycle.

Trishaws were already popular by then, thanks to the petrol-scarce war years and the waning popularity of rickshaws, which were considered inhumane and not befitting the image of a modern society. In Singapore, the trishaw bicycles were attached to the side of the carriage but elsewhere in Asia, the bicycles were attached to the back of the carriage. In Singapore, patrons disliked having the rider in the rear as they felt that it invaded their privacy. But goods and produce had no such sentiments.

San Chwee designed and produced a carriage tricycle that put a wooden platform in front of the rider. Mudguards covered the large 18-inch wheels on either side of the platform. The size of the tyres determined the load that the carriage tricycle could bear. Most bicycles used wheels that were 16 to 18 inches in size. Trishaws used 18-inch ones. As these workhorses were often used to move heavy goods such as water, rice and other bulky items, San Chwee used larger wheels. Each mudguard bore delicate, hand-drawn gold designs. Robert's most vivid memory of the time was watching the workers dip a fine brush into a mixture of gold powder and quick-dry solution and drawing neat, straight lines freehand. Robert marvelled at the precision and confidence of the craftsmen. There were no erasers and, thus, no room for mistakes.

San Chwee's innovation was a hit with the market traders, and soon, San Chwee had a booking list that was several months' long. Production was slow, however, as each unit had

---

25   PictureSG, National Library Board

to be shaped, assembled, and finished by hand. Robert recalls that Ban Hock Hin could produce only about eight to ten units each month.

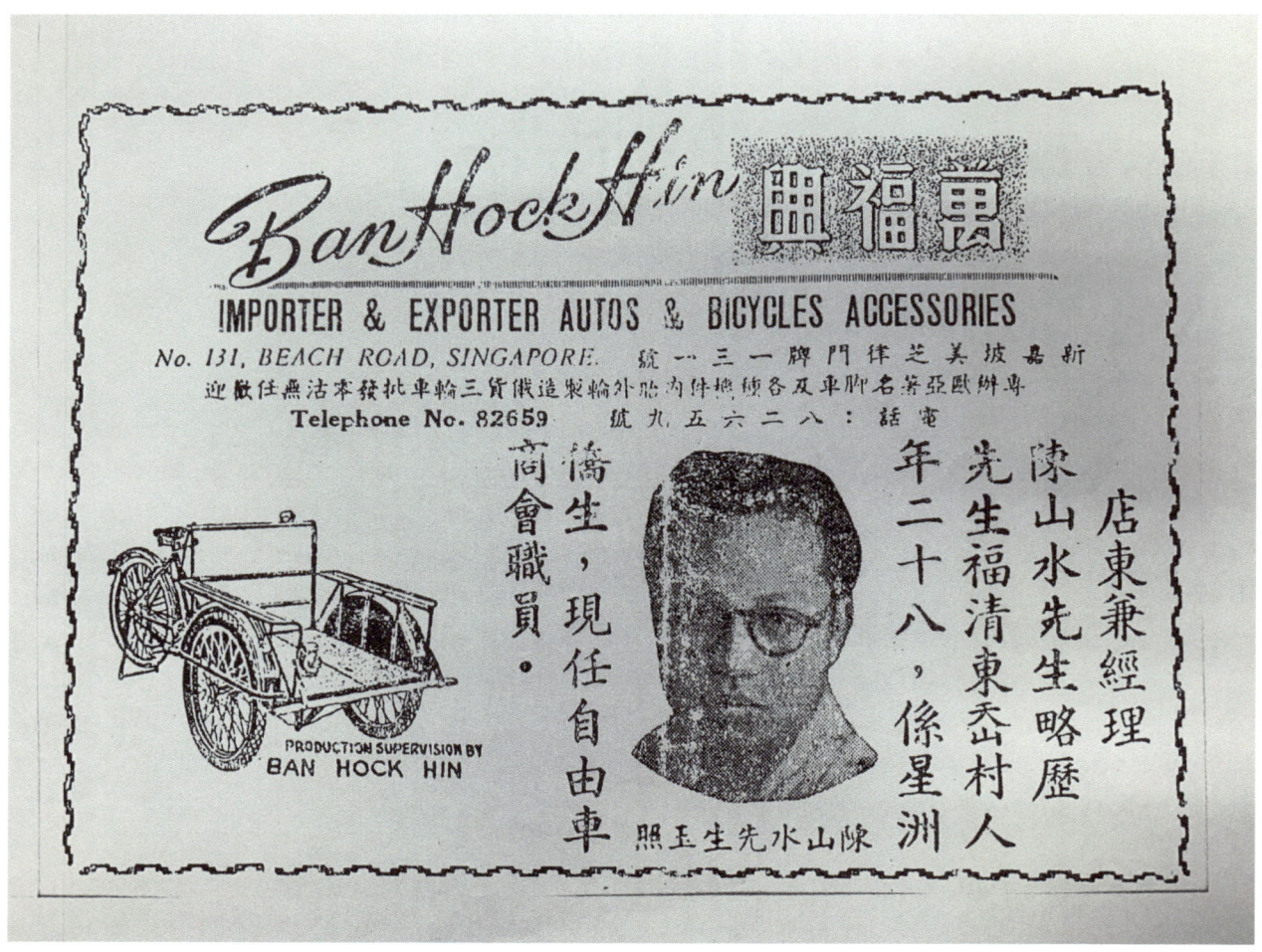

Ban Hock Hin advertisement featuring San Chwee's carriage tricycle circa 1948. It introduces Tan San Chwee, the owner-manager, as a local-born overseas Chinese from Fuqing province, Dong Ao village. It also identifies him as a committee member of the bicycle association. The Chinese text also mentions that he deals with European and Asian brands of bicycles.

As demand for the carriage tricycle picked up, so did San Chwee's need for labour. As was still fairly common practice at the time, he wrote home to his father's village of Dong Ao to invite help from his clansmen. Clansmen were preferred not only because it was easy to communicate in the same language, but also because everyone in the clan was, in some way or other, related. One could rely on a fellow clansman to be loyal and hardworking – anything less would be a huge disgrace to his elders back home where everyone in the village knew everyone else. Moreover, the villagers considered an opportunity to work overseas akin to striking the lottery. These rare opportunities were greatly cherished, and the lucky ones knew they bore the hopes and dreams of all their loved ones and the rest of the villagers with them. Although life abroad would be hard and lean, it was still a great deal better than the barrenness of village life. At the very least, it was pregnant with potential and promise.

Once in Singapore, they could expect a place to sleep, three meals a day, and plenty of hard labour. San Chwee paid his labourers about $10 to $12 a month. Everyone would sleep on the shop floor. Each person had a foldable canvas bed. At night, the shop would turn into a dormitory with rows of canvas beds. In the daytime, these flimsy things would be folded, with the thin pillows and blankets tucked inside the folds, then hung up by their legs. Robert remembers sleeping in the shop with the rest of the workers when he worked in the shop as a child.

San Chwee eventually had 10 to 20 workers help him with the production of these carriage tricycles. Initially, the crew would cut and shape the metal frame for the carriage tricycles in-house. As demand intensified, San Chwee outsourced the job to metal shops and focused on assembling and finishing the vehicles. Space at 131 Beach Road also grew cramped as his family and business grew. San Chwee then rented a second shophouse unit a few doors down from Ban Hock Hin and moved his family there to free up the second floor for his business needs. Ever entrepreneurial, he sublet the lower unit of the new premises to a provision store called Kian Huat while the family lived upstairs.

With the income and profit from making carriage tricycles, San Chwee could further expand the business. He began to import and export bicycles. The premium bicycle brand of the time was the UK-made Raleigh. However, the same manufacturer also produced a mid-range brand called Rudge, which Ban Hock Hin imported as an official agent. The company also imported BSA and Hercule direct from the UK. Robert recalls that these bicycle brands would appoint local sales representatives who would take orders from the larger bicycle shops such as Ban Hock Hin. The sales representatives would earn commission on the orders. These larger bicycle shops would then sell to smaller bicycle shops who couldn't afford to place big orders and therefore could not deal directly with the sales representatives. Ban Hock Hin grew to become one of the three largest bicycle importers in Singapore. The other two – Sing Huat and Ban Hong Chan – were also Henghua-owned.

Ban Hock Hin did not focus on local business alone, however. From the latter half of the 1940s through to the 1950s, San Chwee imported bicycles in bulk and re-exported them in smaller batches to Malaya, Indonesia, Borneo, and the Philippines. He cultivated his export opportunities through his clan connections throughout the region as the Henghua dominated the transport industry not only in Singapore, but also in other Southeast Asian countries. As a result, business was good. Robert estimates that Ban Hock Hin exported nearly a thousand units of bicycles a year. But competition in the trade was brutal, and profits were paper-thin. Thus, San Chwee had to find unconventional resources and solutions to turn in a decent profit.

For example, despite the volume of trade that Ban Hock Hin was doing, the business didn't have a warehouse to store or a workspace to assemble the large shipments of bicycles. Instead, Bee Bee remembers small armies of workers congregating in the streets outside 131 Beach Road at night to unpack the crates of parts, assemble the bicycles, and repack them for redistribution. Once traffic died with the close of the business day, the deserted roads became free workspaces for San Chwee's business. By the time the sun rose the next day and vehicles started taking to the streets, San Chwee's bicycles would be ready for export and redistribution.

Business then relied heavily on trust, not contracts. San Chwee would give his overseas customers credit of 60 to 90 days, and his customers would travel personally to Singapore to pay him in cash and to place additional orders. When they couldn't do so, they'd have a trusted associate do so for them. There were times San Chwee would travel to collect the monies himself.

San Chwee was a hard worker. Ban Hock Hin closed only three days each year, and those were the first three days of the Lunar New Year. For the rest of the year, however, the shop would open for business at 7 in the morning and shut only at 9 at night. The workers ate all their meals at the shop. Initially, San Chwee's mother, known to the family as Zhu Jiak Ma (grandma who cooks) or Lai Ma, was responsible for cooking those meals but later, Ah Yee took over. Eventually, San Chwee employed a cook to prepare food. Workers would eat in two sittings. Robert remembers them scarfing down large bowls of rice, but the accompanying dishes were hearty too. He recalls having vegetables but also chicken, pork, and even fish and prawn. In true coolie form, the men would eat either while squatting or while sitting with one foot on the bench. This must've been a comfortable position because a few of Robert's grandchildren – born some 70 years later – would be found eating with one foot on the chair when they were young.

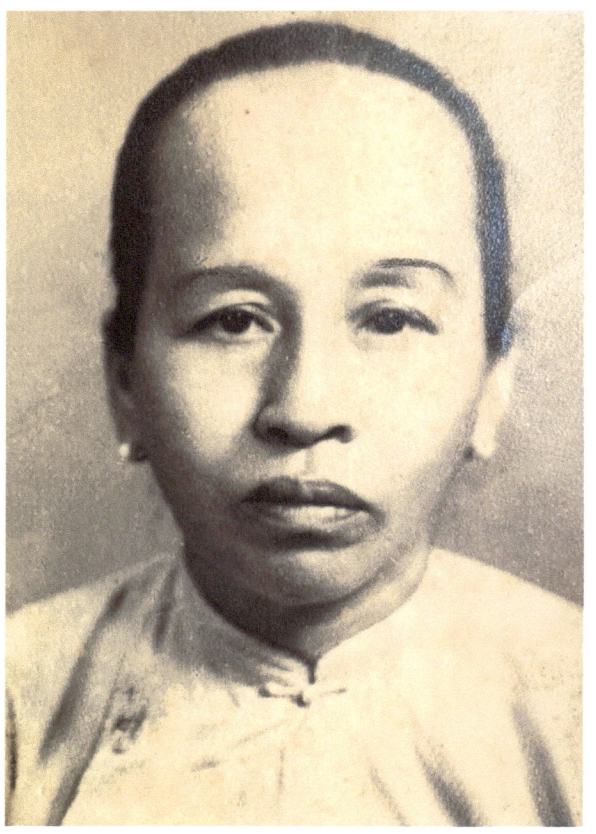

San Chwee's mother who is known as Zhu Jiak Ma to family members because she did a lot of cooking for the business and family.

By the late 1940s, San Chwee did well enough that he could buy 10,000 square feet of land in Geylang, and he built a large bungalow on it. When the bungalow at 24 Geylang Lorong 9 was completed in 1950, he moved his family out of the cramped living space above Ban Hock Hin into their spacious new home. The next year, San Chwee celebrated the birth of his youngest son, Kah Chuan (Richard). Richard, incidentally, was the only one of San Chwee's children to have been born in a hospital – the others were all born at home with the help of midwives.

The grounds were large enough for San Chwee to host a lavish wedding party for his youngest brother Tan Kim Chwee. The bungalow was big enough to accommodate Kim Chwee and his new wife for a while. Kim Chwee helped his older brother out at Ban Hock Hin for a while. Unfortunately, San Chwee and Kim Chwee fell out a few years later. Singapore in the early 1950s was rife with strikes and protests by workers. Ban Hock Hin's workers held a demonstration outside the shop and even threw black oil on the business' signboard, which was considered a terrible insult. Kim Chwee had sided with the workers. Livid, San Chwee had his young brother move out and go his own way. It seems Kim Chwee then turned to trishaw riding for a living.

By this time, San Chwee was wealthy enough to indulge in all manner of distractions, many of them being women. He had taken on another woman and set her up in a shophouse in Tessensohn Road. Her name was Kim Hiok, and she bore San Chwee a son, Siew Chuan. Although he had arranged for her to live separately from the main family, she was no stranger to them. She served the customary tea to Kim Lian, acknowledging her as the primary wife, and thus, she was accepted as a legitimate part of the family. Bee Bee remembers everyone going for family outings together, sometimes to Katong Park and sometimes to Haw Par Villa.

The extended Tan family at the spacious home at 24 Geylang Lorong 9. Circa 1952.
Back row, from left to right: Cheng Bee, Bee Chuan (Robert), Cheng Jin.
Front row, from left to right: Chin Bee (Diane), Bee Bee, Kim Hiok, Kim Lian, Nyonya Ma, Kah Chuan (Richard), San Chwee, Ah Yee, Siew Bee (Rosey), and Cheng Chuan (Harry).

However, when San Chwee started another serious relationship with a woman called Mary, Kim Hiok disappeared, taking her son with her. San Chwee took pains to find them, and he even took out advertisements offering a reward for information on their whereabouts but to no avail. Mary went on to give San Chwee three daughters. At some point in the 1950s, Ah Yee opted to move out of Geylang and live on the third floor of Ban Hock Hin.

Although Ban Hock Hin's business seemed to be booming in the 1950s, trouble was not far off. Distractions took San Chwee's attention off his business. Without proper management, processes and reliable staff, Ban Hock Hin soon ran into financial difficulties and had to stop the regional import-export trade by the end of the 1950s. Instead, it returned to its roots in repairs and sales to the end users until new technology and products created an exciting new market in the 1960s.

1940s to 1960s: Robert

Growing Up

Note on name use: Bee Chuan didn't adopt the name 'Robert' until his teenage years. Hence, I generally use the name that he went by at the time of the events being recounted, meaning I refer to him as 'Yin Jio' when talking about childhood events, 'Bee Chuan' when recounting his school years, and 'Robert' when talking about events that occur after he adopts the English name. The only time that changes is when I refer to the present-day person recollecting the past, at which point I use the name he goes by at the time of writing, which is 'Robert'.

Robert was given the name Bee Chuan at birth, and Bee Chuan was a sickly child in his early years. In Chinese fashion, his elders decided to give him a nickname that they hoped would fend off misfortune. They picked *Yin Jio* or 'hard rock'. In hindsight, perhaps this nickname was aptly chosen. Half a century later, Robert would suffer a bad fall in which he hit his head hard against a bathroom sink. The porcelain sink broke; his head didn't.

As San Chwee's eldest son, Yin Jio was raised with the idea that one day, Ban Hock Hin would be his responsibility. Thus, his training in business started early.

Robert recalls being summoned to work at Ban Hock Hin at a young age. One day when he was nine or 10, his father told him, "*Lai, lai, lai. Kee gor diam.*" (Come, come, come. Go mind the store.) And from then on, Bee Chuan would spend every school holiday at the shop. Bee Chuan's first job was to collect money. He'd sit at a simple wooden table with drawers under the staircase that led to the second floor of the shophouse. In the drawer was a daily collection sheet where he'd record the amounts he'd collect from customers. If the customer was able to provide an invoice number, he'd write that down too. But not everybody had invoice numbers to give. There simply was no proper system of recording sales – or any other business process. This failure to set up proper systems and accounting stymied Ban Hock Hin's growth under San Chwee and contributed to the business' decline in the late 1950s.

He recalls that while other children were enjoying carefree school holidays, he would have to mind the shop for all the long hours it was open. When he didn't have anything to do in the shop, he'd read books or walk about and observe the adults at work. Robert also remembers listening to his father and other adults discuss business matters. "The things they were saying didn't have much meaning for me then," he said. "But somehow those things they discussed registered in my mind, and eventually, they started to make sense. Those meaningless words became knowledge, and that knowledge benefitted me." When Robert had children of his own, he would adopt this training approach by bringing them along to his dinners with clients and business associates.

His early business education also armed him with a skill no one else in his family picked up – the Henghua language. Henghua was the language of the transport trade but Hokkien was the more commonly used language of trade in general. San Chwee had to learn Hokkien, as well as Malay, to communicate with his customers. Bee Bee recalls that he and Zhu Jiak Ma, who was Henghua, spoke Hokkien with a heavy Henghua accent. It was not uncommon for people of the time to speak – at least a smattering of – several dialects and languages in multiracial Singapore.

Kim Lian spoke Hokkien. Because she was responsible for things at home, the children all came to learn their 'Mother Tongue', Hokkien. However, San Chwee and his Henghua workers at Ban Hock Hin spoke Henghua at work. Young Bee Chuan easily picked up his 'Father Tongue' while spending time at the business. Because none of his siblings spent their early years in the shop, they didn't get to learn their 'Father Tongue'.

While Robert's business education started early, his formal one was rather patchy. He remembers Kim Lian taking him and his two elder sisters – Cheng Jin and Cheng Bee – to the Victoria Street Girls' School (precursor to St Nicholas Girls' School on Victoria Street) to register for primary school only to realise that it was an all-girls' school. He was then registered at Catholic High instead. However, it wasn't long before Yin Jio fell sick. Nyonya Ma discerned that the boy fell sick because the school was at odds with the family religion – they were Buddhist, but the school Yin Jio attended was Catholic. The gods must not have been happy with the arrangement. Hence, Yin Jio was withdrawn from Catholic High and registered with Tao Nan instead.

Things at Tao Nan didn't go all that smoothly either. While he was playing in the schoolyard, some children dropped a broken brick on Yin Jio's head. He remembers there being a great deal of blood, and a huge fuss ensued. He was withdrawn from school. About a year later, the elders thought to give school another go. Seeing that Yin Jio didn't have much luck with schools bearing a religious affiliation, they thought that perhaps the Mercantile School on Middle Road would be more suitable. As luck would have it, Yin Jio came down with appendicitis and had to be rushed to the hospital in agony. He remembers that the bloating following the first operation was so severe the doctors nearly wanted to operate again. Luckily, he passed wind, which alleviated the pain and bloating, and he avoided going under the knife a second time. Again, the elders took it as sign that school wasn't quite the place for Yin Jio and pulled him out.

Yin Jio spent another year without formal education. Instead, his mother took him along to her card games. One of Kim Lian's friends' daughters noticed the eight-year-old attending her mother's card parties instead of school. She herself was educated at an English school and understood the value of education, especially for boys who were expected to work and earn income when they grew up. She persuaded Kim Lian to put Yin Jio back in school and used her friendship with the principal of Gan Eng Seng to help him get a place in Primary Two. Yin Jio had not completed Primary One and was, by then, over-aged for that level.

This time, school took. Yin Jio excelled academically and regularly topped his class. He learned English and dropped the use of his childhood nickname, Yin Jio, switching to his formal name, Bee Chuan, instead. The Secondary School Entrance Exams (precursor to the Primary School Leaving Exam) was a cinch for him and he did well.

After the PSLE, Bee Chuan was placed in Outram Secondary school. But within the first year, a group of students – including Bee Chuan – were moved to the newly opened Pasir Panjang Secondary School. In Secondary Two, he and another group of students were transferred to Siglap Secondary School. At Siglap Secondary, Bee Chuan continued to do well, again topping his class and excelling in Math and Science. It was also during this time that he adopted the English name, Robert. He saw that others had English names and wanted one for himself. But he also needed it to be easy to write and to pronounce. Hence, he chose 'Robert'. Family members continued to call him Tua Chuan (Big Chuan) in a nod to his status as the eldest son in the family. The other two sons were known as Cheng Chuan (Harry), or Suey Chuan (Little Chuan), and Kah Chuan (Richard).

The teenage Robert was no studious bookworm as his mischievous streak endured throughout secondary school. He remembers an incident during Science class where a Bunsen burner went missing. As everyone was searching for the missing equipment, Robert yelled out, "I found it! I found it!" When his classmates rushed over to look at his 'find', Robert gleefully showed them a vulgar hand signal. Unfortunately for him, his form teacher was among those who had rushed over. Robert was made to stand on the desk for the rest of the class as punishment.

Despite his penchant for pranks, Robert did so well that in Secondary Three, he was transferred to the 'A' class where the students were groomed for academic excellence, and his academic future looked bright. However, it was at this juncture that things at home would drive Robert to a fateful decision.

Robert (third from left) conducting a science experiment in Form Three in Siglap Secondary School. A bright student, he was placed in the 'A' class.

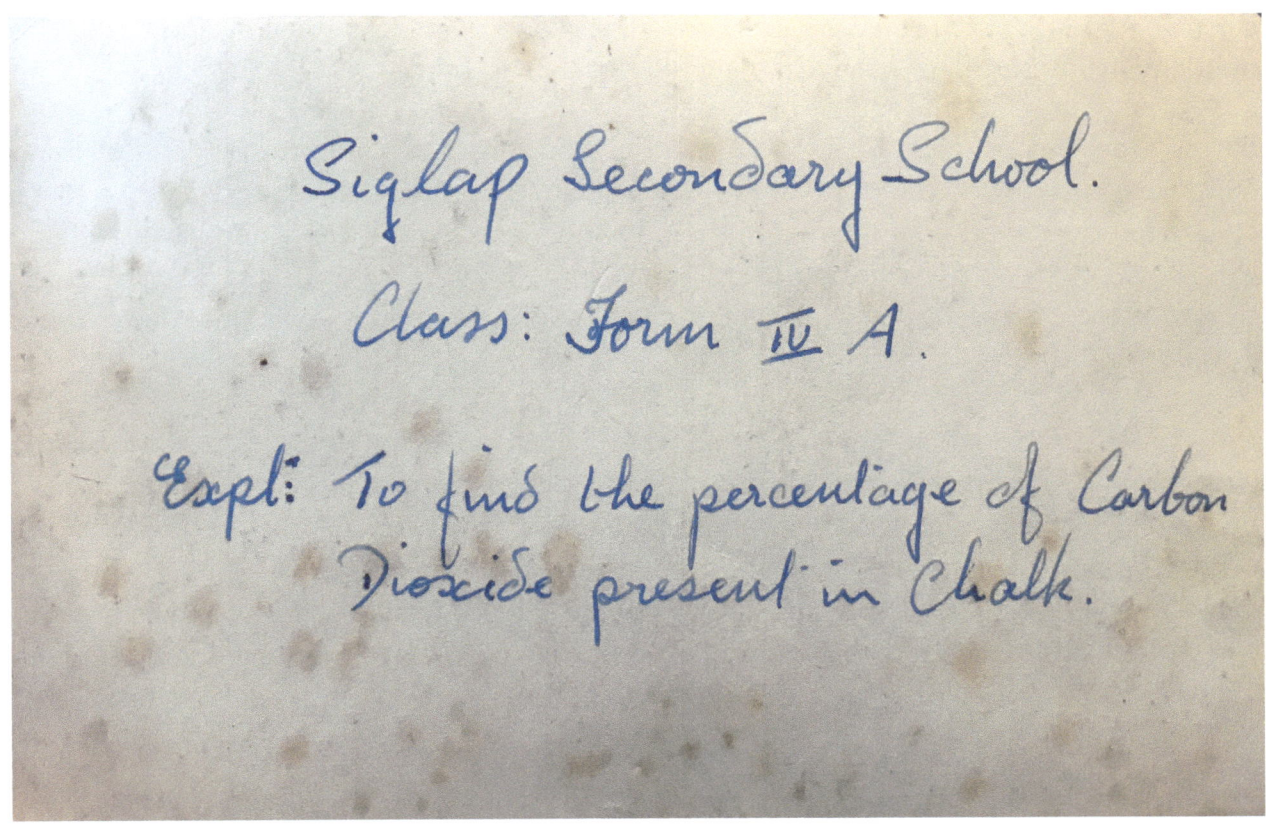

The writing on the back of the above photo of Robert in the science lab.

San Chwee and Kim Lian's relationship was a turbulent one. Kim Lian's family heaped scorn on San Chwee when he was young and poor, and it didn't seem like the relationships improved much even after San Chwee prospered.

By the 1950s, San Chwee had already proven himself a capable self-made man. Although not quite a tycoon, he was certainly considered a successful *towkay*. Kim Lian's family's fortunes were decidedly reversed by this time. Kim Lian's Peranakan brother-in-law had fallen hard from his wealthy perch, and her sister's family was near destitute. Robert remembers them living in a small attic space on Cecil Street. Kim Lian was now the sibling with means, and she would squirrel away baskets full of supplies and quietly hand them to her impoverished elder sister. San Chwee was livid when he found out.

Husband and wife would also row whenever it came time for San Chwee to give Kim Lian money for the monthly household expenses. Neither appreciated the other's lifestyle, and they couldn't seem to see eye-to-eye on anything. It didn't help that both were strong-willed and outspoken, unafraid to press a point.

While Robert inherited his parents' strong will and fiery tempers, he hated the constant quarrelling between them, and the chaos that came from a house crowded with children. By this time in the latter half of the 1950s, all of Robert's siblings had been born and most were running around as young children or teens. His siblings remember him as being quite stern and serious; Robert always liked orderliness and quiet, and the Geylang home was neither. Furthermore, he wasn't particularly close to his parents.

San Chwee was a hands-off kind of parent. Aside from providing housing and living expenses, San Chwee did not engage with his family very much. He hardly spoke to his children and showed little interest in them or their education, even when his eldest son was proving himself quite the scholar. Disappointed in his father's lack of interest, vexed by his parents' frequent fights, and increasingly confident in his own abilities, 17-year-old Robert started to yearn for independence.

After one heated exchange with his dad when he was in Form Three, Robert left home. In the post-war years, talk of self-government for Singapore had gained momentum. In preparation for Singapore's self-government, the First Singapore Infantry Regiment (1 SIR) was formed on 12 March 1957[26]. The army had been advertising widely – even in schools – for recruits. Robert was already in a uniformed group, the Cadet Corp, and the discipline and orderliness of it suited him. He also liked how smart the army uniforms looked in the posters. More importantly, the army looked to him like a good way to quickly establish a career for himself.

Eileen Tan @ Eileen Aung-Thwin

---

[26]   http://www.nas.gov.sg/archivesonline/data/pdfdoc/MINDEF_20070709001/MINDEF_20070709002.pdf

A good friend of his was also keen on enlisting so they did it together. At the time of enlistment, however, Robert was a few months short of the legal recruitment age of 18, but he scored very well in the entrance exams, which presented a conundrum for the recruitment officers. After some deliberation with a British officer, however, the army accepted Robert into its ranks. He was one of only 237 who were accepted out of 1,420 applicants[27]. He signed a five-year contract with them and was looking forward to starting his new life of independence.

Once enlisted, however, he was greatly dismayed to find that some of the Non-Commissioned Officers bore gang tattoos. The government had been cracking down on secret societies, and it seemed to Robert that perhaps some gangsters might have sought sanctuary from prosecution for their crimes by joining the army. In the military, only military police and military courts meted out justice. So long as the gang – or former gang – members didn't break military law, they would not be held accountable for any illegal activities they might have engaged in before they joined the army. Therefore, these men could start life with a 'clean slate' of sorts. However, that didn't necessarily mean that their territorial ways were behind them.

During those years, secret societies and gangs were rife. The notorious gangs were 08, 24, 369, and 18. Each gang had their colours and numbers too. Street wars were not uncommon. Coffeeshop conversations could turn on a phrase into a tussle. Gangsters were present everywhere, even in secondary schools. Robert had always been careful to avoid seeking favours or protection from these dangerous elements – he knew that the moment he did, he'd be unable to extricate himself. Instead, he had made sure to stay at a friendly distance from them. He had already witnessed them fighting and using weapons with unsettling violence. Hence, he was dismayed to find himself under the authority of some NCOs who bore gang tattoos. He feared that eventually he'd be drawn into gang and turf wars.

Back at home, Kim Lian wasn't so quick to let her eldest son go. When Robert's parents found the farewell note he left them, Kim Lian hunted down her wayward son. When she found him two months after he'd left home, she told him, "*Ho ti mm pak teng; ho kia mm tng peng!*" meaning good metal isn't used to hammer nails and good sons don't join the army. Her words struck home with Robert, especially as he had just seen the elements in the army that he'd have to deal with. But there remained the little matter of the contract Robert had signed with the army. Kim Lian wrote to the army authorities with the help of a letter writer to seek Robert's discharge from the army. Given that he had been underaged when he signed on without parental consent, the army released him quickly. However, he had to appear in front of a military court to answer for his change of mind. Robert muses that if it hadn't been for the tattooed NCOs, he likely would have stayed in the military.

---

[27] http://www.nas.gov.sg/archivesonline/data/pdfdoc/MINDEF_20070709001/MINDEF_20070709002.pdf

Robert (second from the right) around the age he enlisted, circa 1957, posing with his buddies. He was 17.

After that episode, Robert never returned to school. Siglap would not accept him back; he'd been overaged to begin with. Instead, he looked for a job. As his relationship with his father was still a little raw, he opted not to work for Ban Hock Hin. He saw an advertisement in the newspaper for a store hand by British retailer, John Little. He applied and got the job. Thus in 1957, at the age of 18, Robert started his career working at John Little's store in Raffles Place. He worked there as a store hand for about two years before he was called home to help with the business.

In the 1950s, San Chwee was supplying bicycles to smaller bicycle retailers. One of them was a shop called Chin Lee on Hill Street, next to the fire station. The owner, Mr Ng, had run into financial difficulties and couldn't pay San Chwee what he owed. Instead, he handed the shop over to San Chwee as payment instead. Ban Hock Hin wasn't doing so well by the late 1950s and had scaled its operations down to retail and repair, having given up its export business. Therefore, San Chwee needed to mind the business a little more closely. Since San Chwee was busy minding Ban Hock Hin, he needed reliable people to run Chin Lee for him. Thus, in 1959, San Chwee asked Robert to manage Chin Lee with his younger brother, Harry. At that time, Robert was 20, and Harry, 16.

When the brothers took over Chin Lee, it was mainly a bicycle retailer. The neighbouring shop sold children's toy cars, tricycles and other toys. Those products looked interesting, so the young men added those products to their portfolio too. Those UK-made products turned out to be a big hit with the customers. The Pedigree brand was very popular, and it had a wide range of products. The brothers even sold Singer sewing machines, and Robert learned to repair them as well. As with Ban Hock Hin, Chin Lee's hours were also 7 a.m. to 9 p.m.

Given the long retail hours, Robert decided to stay in the residential space about Chin Lee. Because Ban Hock Hin's business was doing poorly in the late 1950s, San Chwee decided to move everyone out of the Geylang bungalow, which was too expensive to maintain. He rented it out for a while and later used it for his second-hand car business. Kim Lian and her children moved to Chin Lee with Robert and Harry. San Chwee and Mary moved to Ban Hock Hin.

Richard remembers the Chin Lee home to be very simple and crowded – one large bedroom sat near the front of the building facing the street. Everyone would sleep there on the floor. A few years later, when Richard was 14, San Chwee bought a one-bedroom HDB flat in Commonwealth Avenue for Kim Lian. Richard moved there with his mom and his sisters, Rosey and Diane.

Training wheels

Robert learned the ropes of running a business at Chin Lee for five years. He grew restless when he realised that there was nothing more for him to learn while running a small retail business. Hence, when an opportunity came up for him to try new things, he took it. He joined an import and export firm called Chu Cheong Pte Ltd in 1962. The *towkay*, Ng Chit Cheong, was an old friend of San Chwee. Hence, when Robert expressed an interest in looking for a job, Mr Ng took him in. Chu Cheong's business networks extended throughout Sabah and Sarawak, and Robert travelled widely in those territories to sell the company's products and to collect orders from customers. It traded in bicycles, spare parts and even sewing machines.

On his first visit to Sabah and Sarawak, he visited Kuching, Sibu, Mili, Kualabilat, Jesselton, Dahat Dato, and Kudat. He also visited Brunei on that trip. He made the month-long journey by boat to Sabah, then by car within the territory, and even by river boat.

In 1964, the manager at Chu Cheong left the company to pursue his ambition of running his own business. He persuaded Robert to join him as a product representative. Therefore, Robert left Chu Cheong, but his new job didn't last long. Robert quickly saw that the new setup didn't have what it took to succeed in representing products in Singapore, so he started looking around for other opportunities.

He saw an advertisement in the papers for a sales position at the newly opened Bridgestone tyre company and applied for it. He made a good impression on the Japanese and was one of two finalists for the job. The other finalist also was Henghua, and his father ran a bicycle shop too. However, the other candidate didn't speak Henghua; he spoke his mother's tongue, Teochew. For the final cut, however, the other man got the job. Robert figures it was likely because he was a university graduate, but Robert had only Form Two qualifications.

Two weeks later, however, Robert received a letter from Bridgestone offering him a position in the purchasing department. The Japanese head of sales, Mino-san, had interviewed Robert and was impressed with him and the potential he saw in the 25-year-old. He encouraged Robert to join the purchasing department first, and when more positions opened in the sales department, he could ask for a transfer. Thus, Robert began a work experience that he would come to see as one of the best of his life.

When Robert joined Bridgestone's purchasing department in a position equivalent to an assistant clerk, the company had just started building a factory in Singapore. There was thus a great deal of equipment and materials that it needed to acquire. The delivery of these goods had to be timed to coincide with the different stages of construction. Late delivery of materials would lead to construction delays and other problems. When Robert first showed up at work, he found piles and piles of unorganised files. He began by organising them according to the actions needed, deadlines, and so on. He then methodically whittled away at outstanding tasks. This organised and systematic approach to his work would characterise Robert's approach to tackling difficult management issues throughout his career.

Robert also found that delays and late deliveries were a common problem. However, faced with his honed-in-the-streets bullshit detector and tough-as-nails approach, suppliers were no longer able to give Bridgestone the run-around. He'd call for a tender and award the contract to suppliers who could deliver the fastest. This sent a signal to other suppliers that Bridgestone prioritised speed and timely deliveries. He warned them that any delivery delays would land them on Bridgestone's blacklist. Each supplier received only one pass for late delivery – anyone who missed a deadline a second time would get blacklisted. In his time with the purchasing department, Robert proposed that a few of the suppliers be blacklisted. Uno-san, the head of purchasing, accepted Robert's recommendations without question.

Aside from setting tough conditions for suppliers, Robert also left nothing to chance. Two weeks before any delivery was due, he'd start putting pressure on the suppliers to ensure they would deliver on time. This kind of close monitoring and strict management meant that all of Robert's contracts were fulfilled on time. Within two months of Robert's involvement, delays disappeared, and the deliveries started to come in ahead of the construction schedule. Other departments in Bridgestone noticed and started to get Robert to help manage their tenders and contracts. Instead of turning away these extra assignments, Robert accepted them as opportunities to build more experience and ended up working until 8 or 9 p.m. every night. Although his salary was a meagre $300 a month, he never claimed overtime for the extra work. A large Malaysian supplier also noticed Robert's influence in the purchasing department and tried to bribe him with a significant sum of money. Robert reported the bribery attempt to his manager instead.

Robert working in the Bridgestone Singapore office. He came to see his time with the Japanese company as one of the best working and learning experiences of his life. He was also highly valued by his Japanese employers because of his work ethic and problem-solving abilities. Circa 1966.

Robert's efforts contributed to the timely completion of Bridgestone's factory. He then found himself freed of purchasing duties. As he'd been promised, the management transferred him to sales. But first, Robert needed to undergo a six-month training in the technical service department. At the end of his six-month stint, however, the technical service department head refused to part with him. "We'll release him when you find another Robert Tan for us," he told sales.

While at the technical service department, Robert was trained in and tasked with technical investigations. One of his duties was to assess tyre claims from all the dealers in Malaysia. He'd have to test the tyres, compile a report, recommend a course of action – whether to compensate and if so, how much – and justify his recommendations. The work was demanding, and the conditions could be brutal.

In one case, Bridgestone tyres used on timber trucks had an unusual problem – the tread on the tyres kept separating and the tyres would eventually burst. The same tyres used on trucks in other industries did not have the same issue. Robert was sent to investigate and to collect data.

For weeks, he had to wake up at 4 a.m. to make his way to the timber truck driver's home. From there, he'd tail the truck driver to the timber forest in Johor, which was a 5-hour drive. He'd observe and record how the truck was used, what surfaces it travelled, how timber was loaded and unloaded, how much weight it bore, and even the times of day that every activity was carried out. He'd record the amount of time and distance the truck travelled between breaks. When the truck stopped, Robert would measure the internal temperatures of the tyre and plot his findings on a graph. He'd even have to climb under the truck, sandwiching himself between the heated truck and tarmac, to obtain his data. The searing heat of the tropical sun combined with that generated by friction and load drove temperatures in the tyres to nearly 100 degrees Celsius. The job was so tough that one of his colleagues was nearly in tears at the thought of having to do it.

Robert carried out similar investigations in timber forests in Pahang, Trengganu and other parts of Malaysia. The technical department then used the data he collected to study rubber compounds, tread patterns and other factors in order to design tyres that were more durable and fit for purpose.

This kind of exercise taught Robert the ins and outs of detailed data collection. Much of Robert's later career would have him put this knowledge about collecting, organising and using data to effective use.

Robert sitting on timber logs during one of his trips to the timber forest in Malaysia to conduct tyre performance investigations. Since cameras were not always available, Robert would sketch pictures and diagrams to include in his reports. Circa 1966.

Robert washing off the dust and sweat after trailing timber trucks to collect data about their tyre usage. He had to brave long days and searing heat to get the job done. Circa 1966.

Robert also recalls another deeply memorable assignment.

Bridgestone supplied tyre inner tubes to the Singapore Traction Company (STC), but the tubes kept leaking. Robert had to conduct tests to determine the cause of the leaks. At the time, STC was using two vehicle brands. Robert's investigations found that one of those brands had a wheel and brake design flaw that caused the inner tubes to overheat and age prematurely.

Robert's report on his findings was forwarded by his superiors to Bridgestone's headquarters in Japan and STC. Unfortunately, the unedited report named both vehicle brands. This oversight resulted in a huge row and red faces among all the companies involved.

The managing director (MD) at STC, Mr Michael Jensen, asked to see the author of the report. Robert was expecting an interrogation, but the conversation didn't go the way he expected. Robert remembers being awed by Mr Jensen's large and fancy office at Mackenzie Road, near the old Rex theatre. However, instead of the grilling Robert expected, he encountered a different line of questioning. Mr Jensen unrolled engineering schematics for the vehicle wheels and brakes, and asked Robert to pinpoint the design flaw that was causing the leaks. Robert didn't even have 'O' Level qualifications, much less an engineering degree. He had no idea how to answer Mr Jensen. So, he shrugged and told Mr Jensen that he was a tyre man, not an engineer, he didn't know anything about brakes.

In 1968, STC awarded the brand without the tyre leakage problem a $4 million contract to supply buses.

Although Robert didn't have much education, his quick intellect, meticulous nature and intuitive problem-solving talent made him a valuable asset to the Japanese. He was often called to accompany them to meetings, even with clients, and thus, his manager had to present him as something more than a technician. Although he had only Form Two qualifications – he never finished Form Three – the company gave him a name card with 'Technical Service Engineer' as his job title. It didn't come with a matching salary, though.

Because of his competence, he was tasked with many assignments, and earned the nickname of "Busy Tan", a riff on his name, "B C Tan". The locals called him "powerful man". Not only did Robert accompany the Japanese for official duties, he would be invited to socialise with them too. But Robert's performance wasn't all that caught the Japanese's eye. Robert spoke the language of the Chinese who dominated the transport industry – Henghua. As a Henghua himself, he could network better than others who weren't.

One year, the company sent Robert on a study trip to Japan to learn about the operations at headquarters. During his visit there, Robert was to encounter an idea that would become a cornerstone of Ban Hock Hin: the computer. Robert remembers little of that visit to Japan but he does remember the computer, which used cards and was placed in a room by itself. He also remembers being told that the computers were able to print pictures and do the work of human beings. The novelty of the idea caught Robert's attention, but he hadn't imagined at the time that this novel idea would one day become a linchpin of his enterprise.

Although Robert was well appreciated by many of his colleagues and management, politics in a large company was unavoidable. Bridgestone Singapore was a joint venture between Bridgestone Japan and a Malaysian investor. The Japanese company managed sales and operations, but the local partner was responsible for human resources and local appointments. Interestingly, all the desirable positions available to locals went to relatives of the local HR representative. Robert understood that no matter how hard he worked or what valuable contributions he made, he had limited prospects in the company.

To make things worse, Robert had joined the union and even served on the union's management committee. He was vocal about policies he felt were unfair, and he didn't go easy on the local management. Furthermore, he didn't have much educational qualifications. He recognised that all those factors could cap his rise.

In 1968, San Chwee approached Robert to take over Ban Hock Hin. He'd lost his taste for the two-wheeler business, which focused only on retail and repair. The 48-year-old San Chwee had already set up another company called Ban Hock Hin Motor that dealt in second-hand cars and pirate taxis. The crowd he ran with in connection to that business was a far more interesting one to him. Harry was already involved in Ban Hock Hin, but San Chwee wasn't confident that he could keep it going alone. San Chwee told Robert that if he didn't take over the business, he would rather close it down.

Robert was initially lukewarm to his father's proposition. He enjoyed his job at Bridgestone, but he also knew his prospects were limited. If he stayed on, he knew he would be a salaryman the rest of his life. And as one with few educational qualifications, he also knew he'd never get far, no matter how capable he was. Yet, he was entering what he considered the most important and productive years of a man's life. The years between 30 and 45 were crucial career years for a man. He saw that the two-wheeler industry was a lively one in the late 1960s; the potential to do well was there. In that trade, qualifications didn't matter – only brains, guts and gumption did. As the boss of a small company, he'd still have more say over his own fate than as a mere employee of a multinational one.

Hence, in 1968, Robert resigned.

The Japanese managing director, Ideguchi-san, tried hard to retain Robert. Although Robert deeply appreciated his efforts, his mind was made up. He wrote a letter to Ideguchi-san to explain his position. He expressed his love for the company and the job, as well as his appreciation for the support that his Japanese bosses gave him, but his future with Bridgestone was in doubt. The fact remained that human resource matters fell under the purview of the Malaysian camp. Furthermore, it was common Japanese management practice to rotate their managers and senior leadership every few years to different countries, and he knew someday his supporters would leave. He also highlighted that he was now nearly 30 years old – the prime of his life as far as a man's career was concerned. He needed to achieve something for himself, and he planned to return to his family's business to build it as best he could. With that explanation, Ideguchi-san finally accepted Robert's resignation.

In reflection, Robert said that his attitude towards difficulties is what set him apart. Instead of seeing problems as something to be feared and avoided, Robert saw them as opportunities to learn. He often says: "If something is easy, you learn nothing. If something is hard, that's where your chance to learn comes in. Knowledge is wealth." This hunger for knowledge and his "bring it on" attitude came to characterise Robert's approach to work and to business, and played a big part in his success.

Therefore, despite his low educational qualifications, Robert was able to excel and succeed. He said: "Education is important, but it is only a basic foundation. The most essential qualities are confidence in oneself to take up challenges, the determination to overcome difficulties in the pursuit of his goals, and finally, the patience to wait for the outcome. The difference can be large."

The many lessons he learned while at Bridgestone came to serve Robert well when he managed Ban Hock Hin. He saw how a small oversight in the STC case caused such consternation and learned that people and companies' reputations were things you needed to handle with kid-gloves. He learned how data was crucial to research, investigation and decision-making. He also learned how to deal positively with problems and people who made mistakes. It was far more productive to focus on solutions than finding fault. It was even more important to prevent the same mistakes from happening again. He also learned more sophisticated business and management skills from the Japanese compared to when he worked for local businesses.

Robert also admired and learned from the Japanese' social graces and habits. He found the Japanese to be very disciplined and socially conscious – in everything they did they ensured that they minimised inconvenience and discomfort to others. For example, when they used tools in the common area, they made it a point to put it back in the same place so that others could find the tools easily. They didn't litter, and when they drank coffee or smoked, they made it a point to dispose of the cup or cigarette butt in a designated bin. He realised that these habits of discipline and orderliness were found not only in a few; they were common across the organisation. It was culture. And this culture affected the efficiency and productivity of an organisation. It also led to high morale among staff who found pride in working in a well-managed and successful organisation. Robert took this lesson to heart; he would eventually implement many of these ideas in the businesses he managed.

Japanese group behaviour made a deep impression on Robert as it was unlike any that he had ever encountered. He embraced the ideal of Japanese social etiquette and incorporated it into his personal and business life. His understanding of Japanese culture and approach to business would also be an asset to him when he dealt with other Japanese companies on behalf of Ban Hock Hin.

1970s: New Order

Taking Charge

After leaving Bridgestone in 1968, Robert joined Ban Hock Hin. By that time, San Chwee had already switched from selling bicycles to selling motorcycles as sales of the latter had suddenly taken off in the early 1960s.

In the 1950s, Singapore had relatively few motorcycles. The top brands included Triumph, BSA and Royal Enfield, but these European machines were pricey – a 200 cc Triumph cost $1,302[28]. Thus, their sale numbers were small – just 1,909 were registered in 1958 and 2,053 in 1959[29].

But in 1958, Honda launched a new four-stroke motorcycle called the Honda Super Cub or simply, the Honda 50, with a small, 50 cc engine. It was quieter than the more common two-stroke engines, highly fuel efficient (90 km per litre), and easy to operate. They were cheap too – the Honda Cub cost less than $500.

Honda's popularity surged in 1961. That year, the Japanese brand swept the top five places in the lightweight category at the 'Olympics' of Grand Prix motorcycle events – the T.T. (tourist trophy) race at the Isle of Man. Supremacy at the races often translated into supremacy in motorcycle sales.

The popularity of Japanese motorcycles, especially the Honda Cub, skyrocketed. In 1960, there was a total of just 15,362 scooters and motorcycles licensed in Singapore, compared to 59,532 cars and 259,390 bicycles[30]. In 1961, Japanese brands, including Honda, Yamaha, Suzuki and Kawasaki, brought 16,377 machines[31] into Singapore.

Adding to this two-wheeler fervour was the growing popularity of Italian brands such as Vespa and Lambretta. Vespas had bigger engines – 125 cc and 150 cc – and a chic and modern aesthetic. In 1961, the Italians brought in some 12,689 machines valued at $8.8 million – double their 1960 imports.

San Chwee, who owned a high-capacity Triumph motorcycle, was quick to catch the rising wave of scooter and motorcycle popularity. Boon Siew, a Malaysian business dealing in

28   Advertisement, *Singapore Free Press*, 9 November 1960
29   Chan Bong Soo, "Local scooter boom", *The Straits Times*, 29 December 1961, pp 10.
30   "59,532 cars in S'pore", *The Straits Times*, 9 May 1960, pp 5.
31   "Motorcycle imports up", *The Straits Times*, 7 August 1962, pp 14.

truck tyres and other products, distributed the Honda Cub, and Ban Hock Hin became an authorised dealer for Honda in 1962. San Chwee got Chin Lee to switch to selling motorcycles too. Many other bicycle shops also switched to selling motorcycles if they had the capital.

Robert remembers the transition being easy, as selling was simpler back then. As long as you had space to display your products and you had people walking by, you could easily attract enquiries, if not customers. Moreover, the new products came with new auxiliary business opportunities such as accessories and accident repair. The machines were relatively simple constructions, and with some trial and error, Ban Hock Hin's bicycle repairers quickly learned to repair motorcycles too. Within a year, both Ban Hock Hin and Chin Lee completed their transition from the bicycle trade to the motorcycle one.

When Robert joined Ban Hock Hin in 1968, the motorcycle business was well established but things were far from ideal. In a fashion true to his need for data and order, Robert started his career with Ban Hock Hin by taking stock of where things stood. He found that the business was worth $60,000. It had five employees in addition to San Chwee and Harry – four mechanics and one accounts clerk. But he also found that the company's reputation and cash flow had fallen to a state where other businesses would no longer extend credit to Ban Hock Hin. Every transaction had to be paid for in cash.

Although the business – and business environment – had changed over the years, San Chwee's freewheeling way of doing business hadn't. Robert found that his father's business ethics were the opposite of his own. Where Robert prized integrity and accountability, San Chwee delighted in getting the upper hand. Before San Chwee concluded a sale, everything was *boleh, boleh* (can, can)! The moment the sale was made, everything became *tat boleh, tat boleh* (cannot, cannot)! Robert was deeply uncomfortable with his father's methods.

San Chwee also lacked a systematic mind. Records were scant – money, receipts, and bits and pieces of notes would disappear into one of the many pockets on his grey safari shirt. No one knew where things were, possibly not even San Chwee himself. Robert's younger brother Harry had joined Ban Hock Hin a few years before Robert, having done so after San Chwee decided to close Chin Lee and focus on Ban Hock Hin alone. Harry was also a master salesman but in the same vein as his father. Initially, Robert would handle sales in addition to admin. However, there were many occasions where Harry would renege on deals and prices that Robert had agreed on with customers. This led to a lot of conflict, and hence, Robert decided to focus on managing the administration of the business and leave sales to Harry. He understood that the business needed proper systems and management if it were to survive.

First, Robert needed to ensure that all the verbal agreements made between himself, his father and his brother were properly documented. He had a lawyer draw up a contract that laid out the relationship Harry and he had with the company and with San Chwee. The document went into detail about how Robert and Harry would pay San Chwee $600 per month to "lease the goodwill of the business of Ban Hock Hin" and how nett profits would be distributed. San Chwee would get 30 per cent and each of his sons would get 35 per cent. The younger Tans would each draw a $450 monthly allowance. The 1968 contract even laid out the requirement for a "half-yearly partnership Meeting to report the state of affairs and progress of the business". The document included details about the business' nett worth.

AGREEMENT.

THIS AGREEMENT is made on the First day of September One thousand nine hundred and sixty-eight Between TAN SAN CHWEE of No. 131, Beach Road, Singapore (hereinafter referred to as "A") of the first part TAN BEE CHUAN of No. 113-M, Commonwealth Close, Queenstown, Singapore (hereinafter referred to as "B") of the second part and TAN CHENG CHUAN of No. 131, Beach Road, Singapore (hereinafter referred to as "C") of the third part

WHEREAS IT IS UNANIMOUSLY AGREED subject as hereinafter mentioned that "A" will lease the Goodwill of the business of BAN HOCK HIN (hereinafter referred to as "THE COMPANY") together with its Current Assets and both "B" and "C" will accept the lease and agree to pay a rental of $600/- per month to "A" with effect from the date of signing of this Agreement. The Parties "B" and "C" having carefully examined and assessed the value of the business of the Company have agreed unanimously that the working Capital as at the commencement of the said business, that is to say on 1st September, 1968, is $60,000/- being made up of outstanding accounts and stocks and which is clearly shown in the Schedule (hereinafter referred to as "SCHEDULE ONE")

ALL THE PARTIES HAVE FURTHER AGREED that the nett Profits of the business with effect from 1.9.68, if any, shall be divided in the following manners:-

Tan San Chwee.	...	30%
Tan Bee Chuan.	...	35%
Tan Cheng Chuan.	...	35%

Both "B" and "C" hereby covenant with "A" as follows:-

1. To obtain the consent of "A" regarding to the Capital so assessed as shown in Schedule One.

2. To manage the business with equal rights but on major affairs they shall consult with each other before execution.

3. To collect all the outstanding accounts due to the Company and also pay off the Company's Creditors to the best they can.

4. To call for a half-yearly partnership Meeting to report the state of affairs and progress of the business and its 1st Meeting will be provisionally fixed on 15.1.1969. In the event of important matters for decision, an extraordinary Meeting may be convened if 2 of the 3 partners have agreed.

5. No partners are permitted to use the Company's name to stand as Guarantor for any person or persons in any matters.

6. No partners are also allowed to draw any money from the Company for personal benefits except those profit, if any, which they are entitled to draw as unanimously approved by all the partners.

7. Both "B" and "C" shall draw a monthly allowance of $450.00 each for services rendered to the Company and this allowance is to commence on 1.10.68.

8. "A" shall remain an inactive partner and will not interfere with the management of "B" and "C".

9. This Agreement is good for a period of five years commencing from 1.9.68 to 31.8.73.

10. On the expiration of the period of five years, "B" and "C" shall continue in full force and effect and subject to the stipulations and conditions herein contained until either "A" or "B" and "C" shall give

Sample page from the 1968 agreement that San Chwee, Robert and Harry signed.

THIS IS THE SCHEDULE REFERRED TO ABOVE AS "SCHEDULE ONE".

1.	Installment Accounts outstanding.	....		$120,000.00
	Less Bad Debts.	....		35,000.00
				$ 85,000.00
2.	Stock in hands.	....		20,000.00
				$105,000.00

Less Amounts due to Sundry Creditors:-
    (1) Guan Hoe Co. (M) Ltd. $19,000.00
    (2) Boon Siew Ltd.   6,000.00
    (3) Chung Khiaw Bank Ltd. 20,000.00   45,000.00

                                                $ 60,000.00
                                              ===========

The foregoing pages 1 to 3 were translated by the undersigned, LOO CHUNG CHEE, from an Agreement in the Chinese version and which is now annexed hereto for easy reference.

The schedule detailing the value of the business in 1968.

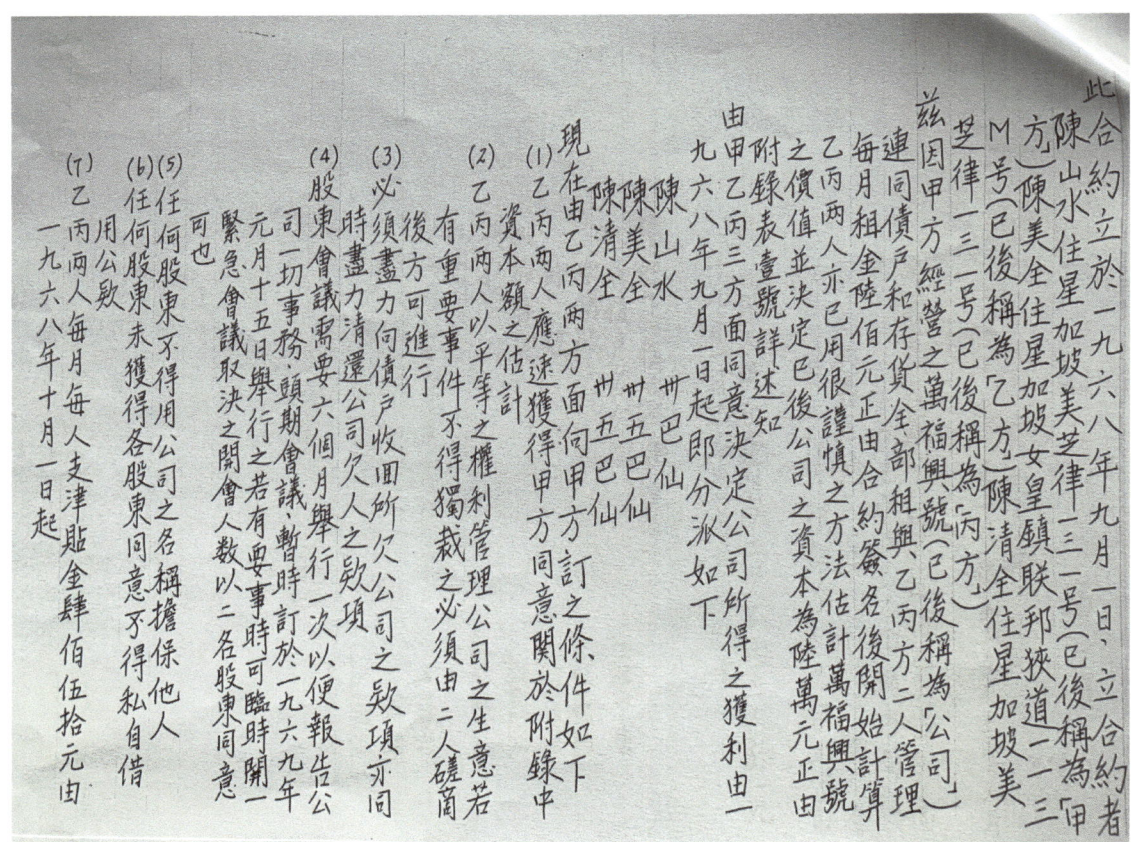

Sample of the Chinese translation of the 1968 agreement.

A few years later, Robert realised that Ban Hock Hin was a sole proprietorship. As a sole proprietorship, the business belonged to San Chwee alone. As a privately incorporated company, all three of them could hold shares and, therefore, own the company. It also presented a more credible business image, something that Robert understood was crucial in the changing business landscape. Robert pushed for the conversion of the business to an incorporated company. San Chwee agreed, and they split the shares equally among all three of them. Ban Hock Hin Co. Pte Ltd was incorporated in 1971.

Next, he set out to reclaim some of Ban Hock Hin's standing in the business community. Robert visited its regular suppliers to explain that Ban Hock Hin was going to do things differently from then on and to persuade them to accept the company's cheques. He promised to issue only cash cheques, not post-dated ones. Some agreed to give Ban Hock Hin a chance.

To ensure that he could indeed honour all cheques and payments, Robert knew he needed to keep a close eye on the company's finances. He said: "For a person, eyes will give you safe passage to see where you are going. For a company, its accounts are the eyes. Without that, the company is blind and can't see where it is going."

To have clear sight of the company's finances, Robert needed a proper system to monitor, manage and account for all revenue and expenses. He introduced payment vouchers – anyone who wanted to spend a cent of company money had to submit a voucher clearly stating the recipient of and the reason for the payment. He also introduced annual performance reviews and financial reports. Robert's youngest sister, Diane (Chin Bee), helped at the business for a time. She recalls that Robert had exacting standards when it came to following procedures and due process, especially when it came to money matters.

He was very strict about keeping company and personal funds separate. All personal expenses had to come from each person's own monthly salary and savings. When the business made money, San Chwee and Harry would want to have the profits shared among the shareholders. But Robert always urged them to reinvest the money into the business. Instead, each of them would get an angpow (bonus) for their efforts. San Chwee and Harry were unhappy with Robert's tough rules, especially when this kind of financial restraint wasn't all that common in their business and social circles of the time. But Robert was unyielding when it came to doing what he thought was right.

Robert's prudence would pay off handsomely. With the financial discipline that he imposed, the company started to regain its footing and its reputation. By 1979, the business value had grown from $60,000 in 1968 to nearly $1 million. It would continue to bloom in the next few decades under Robert's meticulous care.

As financial management systems fell into place, Robert turned his attention to other aspects of the business, namely, the hire purchase accounts. The roaring motorcycle trade brought with it a financing programme that wasn't common in the bicycle trade – the hire purchase (HP) scheme. Although hire purchase arrangements had been around from the turn of the century, it wasn't widespread in the two-wheeler trade until motorcycles became popular. Most of Ban Hock Hin's motorcycle sales were made on hire purchase at a 15 per cent per annum interest rate, which meant that one of the most important assets the company had was its hire purchase records. Under this payment plan, hirers could take up to two years to pay for their motorcycles. Records ensured that the company and the hirer or customer could keep track of the outstanding amount.

Ban Hock Hin kept the details of its HP accounts in five thick, 500-page books. Each HP account had its own page on which to record payments. A separate HP index book recorded the bike number, customer name and the reference number to which of the five large books held the HP details. Each time a customer came to make payment, the clerk had to look up the customer name or bike number in the index book, refer to the HP book, enter the payment details into the correct page, collect payment, and then issue a receipt to the customer. At the end of each day, the clerk had to produce a report of all the collections made that day. This cumbersome system was laborious and time-consuming. It also took up unnecessary space as an entire book had to be retained even if only one or two HP accounts remained outstanding. Robert knew there had to be a better way of doing things.

Therefore, in 1973, Robert adopted the index filing system Kardex to manage the HP records and began the large undertaking of transferring all the HP records to the new filing system. The Kardex records were organised by vehicle registration numbers in alphabetical order, which made it much faster and easier to locate and update HP accounts. The transition took months to complete. But the effort was worth it. A few years later, this move would prove judicious beyond administrative efficiency. It would save the company from ruin.

Rallying the Trade

Even as Robert organised and orchestrated the inner workings of Ban Hock Hin, developments in the motorcycle industry would soon demand that he do the same for the trade.

By the 1970s, Singapore had already started to find its groove after its shock separation from Malaya. The economy was zipping along at an average growth rate of 8 per cent or higher. The country was enjoying nearly full employment and even labour shortages in some sectors[32]. Rapid industrialisation meant that Singapore's army of workers needed affordable and reliable means of transport to help them drive all that economic activity. Yet, the public transport system struggled to meet demand.

Bus commuters in the post-war decades were plagued by overcrowding, corruption, worker strikes, and uncoordinated routes and fares. The poorly maintained, hot and rickety buses frequently broke down. According to the Biblioasia website, it was reported that in early 1974, some 800 out of 1,450[33] buses of the newly formed Singapore Bus Service (SBS) would break down *daily*. The bus industry was in chaos as the government struggled to shore up the deteriorating bus services.

Without reliable bus services, pirate taxis, also known among the Chinese as '*pah ong chia*' or 'tyrant car', grew to be an attractive form of transport. These illegal and unlicensed taxi services were provided by enterprising car owners and became very popular after the Japanese Occupation ended. Pirate taxi fares were negotiated between driver and passenger, and passengers often had to share the taxi with multiple strangers going to different destinations as drivers tried to maximise fares. Many pirate taxis were poorly maintained, and passengers were unprotected by insurance in the event of accidents. Yet, an estimated 12,000 plied the roads in 1965.

The trade seemed so lucrative that even San Chwee dabbled in it. He had a small fleet of about 20 to 30 rickety, second-hand cars which he hired out to drivers. But this enterprise didn't last long as the Government clamped down on pirate taxis with tough

[32] http://factsanddetails.com/southeast-asia/Singapore/sub5_7c/entry-3782.html#chapter-7

[33] Ibid

new legislation in 1970. By 1971, the pirate taxi had gone largely extinct[34]. After that, San Chwee turned to the second-hand car trade.

Between the unreliable bus services and the chaotic pirate taxi scene, Singaporeans in the 1950s and 1960s didn't have much public transport options. Thus, private transport was even more attractive – and one could argue, essential – than ever. Once Japanese motorcycles were introduced to the market in 1960, they became the best option for the working class. Already cheap, Japanese motorcycles were even more affordable because of financing programmes. They gave riders flexibility and control over their routes and timings. They were lightly regulated – riding licences were easy to obtain, and riding helmets weren't even required. Therefore, the motorcycle population mushroomed. In 1960, there were 15,362 motorcycles and scooters on the road. By 1968, there were 85,000.

The explosion in the motorcycle population in the 1960s caused the authorities consternation even as they provided the lower income folks an attractive and affordable means of transport. Motorcycles were light, manoeuvrable, and fast, but inherently unstable. Riders often wove dangerously between bigger vehicles and traffic lanes. The nature of the two-wheeler and the dangerous behaviours of many of its users meant that motorcycle riders were among the most vulnerable of road users.

One of the areas of greatest concern was the high death rates of motorcycle users involved in traffic accidents.

According to a 21 May *Straits Times* article[35], there were 10,349 road casualties in 1967, of which one-third were motorcycle riders or their pillion riders. Most deaths and severe injury were caused by head trauma. National Safety First Council of Singapore ran a campaign from May 17 to June 4 to encourage motorcycle and scooter riders to wear crash helmets[36]. Thousands of posters, banners and letters were used to send riders the message that crash helmets saved lives. The 21 May article also mentioned that a number of calls had been made for legislation to make the wearing of crash helmets compulsory. However, the authorities at the time preferred to encourage the wearing of helmets through publicity and education instead of making it compulsory.

The authorities' restraint didn't last long, however. In August 1969, the government announced legislation on the compulsory use of crash helmets. The Transport Advisory Board's interim report released on 2 August recommended the move, which was immediately accepted by the Minister for Communications, Mr Yong Nyuk Lin. He said the scheme would be introduced in three phases. From 1 November that year, all applicants for the "L" – or provisional – licence had to buy and use helmets as a condition for being

---

[34] Lew Yii Der and Choi Chik Cheong, "Overview of Singapore's Land Transport Development 1965-2015" in Tien Fang Fwa (ed.), *50 Years of Transportation in Singapore: Achievements and Challenges*, Singapore: World Scientific, 2016, pp 141

[35] *The Straits Times,* 21 May 1968, pp 8

[36] *The Straits Times, 4 May 1968, pp 11*

issued the "L" licence; from 1 Feb 1970, all 'L' riders had to wear crash helmets; and finally, from 1 Jan 1971, all riders – regardless of licence type – had to don helmets[37].

It seems the authorities felt legislation was the only way to modify riders' behaviour. In another article two days later, Mr Yong was quoted as saying that safety campaigns had only fleeting effects on helmet use – after the campaign organised by the National Safety First Council of Singapore in the previous year, helmet use increased from 10 per cent to 30 per cent. However, by 1969, that proportion had dropped to 15 per cent. Of the 83 riders killed in 1969, only one had worn a crash helmet – but he hadn't strapped it on securely[38]. The new legislation would affect 105,000 two-wheeler licence holders in Singapore. The machine population stood at 94,000.

News of the crash helmet legislation alarmed Robert. He realised that despite such legislation having serious implications for the motorcycle industry, the trade didn't have any party to represent its interests to the government and other stakeholders; neither did it have any formal mechanism for working together to defend common interests. Even the rickshaw pullers and poor immigrants during Kow Sai's time understood that they had greater safety and negotiating power in numbers and had banded together in associations. The bicycle trade had its own association too.

He thus called for a meeting with a few of the bigger dealers in the industry:

- Auto Trade Corporation Pte Ltd
- Heng Ho Co.
- Hock Motors & Co. Pte Ltd.
- Hin Huat Motor Co.
- Hong Guan Motor Pte Ltd.
- Hong Hin Motor Co.
- Tai Hin Enterprise Co.
- Tiong Hin Motor Co.
- Star Union Co.

Robert represented Ban Hock Hin at the meeting, which was held at 131 Beach Road after retail hours ended at 8 p.m. They were of the same mind that the motorcycle trade needed an association to represent its interests and organise collective action. The news about the helmet legislation had perturbed them all.

As highlighted by Communications Minister Yong, helmet use in the industry was rare – barely 10 to 15 per cent. Not only was wearing a helmet considered inconvenient and uncomfortable, helmets represented an extra cost to the riders, and many of them had difficulty paying for extra accessories. The dealers were also concerned that there weren't enough helmets in the market.

---

[37]   *The Straits Times*, 2 August 1969, pp 8
[38]   "Keeping their heads", *The Straits Times*, 4 August 1969, pp 12

If the implementation of this law was badly executed or badly received by riders, things could go south for the industry. Without helmets, riders couldn't ride their machines, and they might decide to return them to the dealers. If large numbers did so, the implications for the trade would be disastrous – some 70 per cent of bike owners were on the hire purchase scheme.

The dealers present decided they would form a pro tem committee to spearhead the formation of the association. They started to spread the word about the association, and the members told the dealers that anyone who was interested to join the pro tem committee could approach Robert. Not many came forward – everyone knew this was a thankless, time-consuming task. Only the original 10 continued to serve as pro tem committee members. Hong Guan Motor's Lim Kim Yiang served as president; Robert, as Honorary Secretary; and Auto Trade's Lee Seng Choa, as Honorary Treasurer.

One of the pro tem committee members did pull in a key person, though. Lee Bon Leong, founding partner of law firm Lee Bon Leong & Co, agreed to serve as legal advisor to the association pro bono. He helped ensure the association was set up – and later managed – properly according to the requisite laws and regulations. The pro tem committee then submitted its application to form the Association with the Registrar of Societies. On 9 September 1970, the Singapore Motor Cycle Trade Association's (SMCTA) application for registration was approved by the Registrar of Societies.

With this formalisation, the membership campaign began in earnest. Canvassing for members was no small task – there were some 200 businesses in the trade. Back then there was no email for mass mailing or social media channels to publicise on. Even mobile phones didn't yet exist. Every dealer had to be approached in person, and the pro tem committee members all had their own businesses to manage. They split the task up among themselves, visiting the dealers whenever they were able to. Robert remembers visiting the dealers with a membership form in hand. Getting dealers to sign up – as long as it was free – was not difficult. The challenges were yet to come. It took the pro tem committee members months to reach out to the majority of the dealers.

By early 1971, the pro tem committee had rustled up a good number of members, and they called for the association's first general meeting on 14 March 1971. The fledging Association did not have its own premises for the meeting and had to borrow the premises of another association. Ban Hock Hin's address at 131 Beach Road was temporarily used as the Association's mailing address. At this inaugural meeting, the association members elected the SMCTA's first executive committee. Robert was to serve as president and Lim Kim Yiang, as Honorary Secretary.

That first year was a busy one. SMCTA members had agreed at the general meeting that the association needed a base of operations, a home of sorts. The first executive committee meeting was held on 28 May 1971 during which the president, honorary secretary and honorary treasurer were authorised to find and buy a suitable property on behalf of the association.

They then found a two-storey property at 40, Sam Leong Road for $42,000. To secure the purchase, a 10 per cent down payment of $4,200 was needed. Ban Hock Hin made the down payment.

The painful process of raising funds from the members then began. Robert remembers that it was very difficult getting SMCTA members to contribute financially, but in the end, the executive committee received donations from 126 parties for a total sum of $89,800. The biggest contributors were Honda distributor Boon Siew Singapore Pte Ltd and Yamaha distributor Hong Leong Co Pte Ltd with donations of $10,000 each. Today, the property at 40, Sam Leong Road is worth more than $4 million.

Robert went on to lead the SMCTA for some 16 years. After the first term as president, Robert elected to serve as honorary secretary – his rationale is that the secretary was really the one who drove most of the activities and initiatives from behind the scenes. His fiery and impatient nature meant that he liked getting things done – and getting them done fast. The secretary position suited his disposition better. For the next decade and a half, Robert took a very active role in the trade and was often the association's government liaison and media spokesman. Media articles about the motorcycle trade and the association often carried his quotes.

The SMCTA under Robert's leadership liaised with the government on behalf of the industry on numerous issues, ranging from appealing legislative changes on the use of side cars to negotiating for more time for its members to adapt to new laws. It also helped motorcycle and scooter riders to adapt to new legislation that affected them – some of which represented a big threat to the welfare of the trade.

For example, in 1974, the Registry of Vehicles announced a new ruling that required learner motorcyclists to pass the highway code before they could ride on the road. This presented a huge challenge to the industry as many of these riders were illiterate and dialect speaking. The highway code test was conducted in the four official languages of English, Mandarin, Malay, and Tamil – many of these riders didn't know any of these languages. If they couldn't pass the test, they'd be forced off the roads, and they would return their bikes on hire purchase to the traders. Once again, motorcycle dealers faced the prospect of having a huge number of bikes returned to them. But this time, the government had an industry representative in SMCTA to work with when introducing the new law.

The SMCTA was able to represent its various stakeholders' concerns and negotiate for more time for the illiterate riders to comply with the new ruling. To support the motorcyclists and help them prepare for the test, the association conducted free highway code classes[39]. The SMCTA's efforts thus helped the riders ease into complying with the new law and averted a potential crisis for the dealers.

Robert was also instrumental in helping the SMCTA take a crucial step that would pay off handsomely. At the start of the 1980s, the Traffic Police sought the association's help

---

[39]   Singapore Motor Cycle Trade Association 8th Anniversary and Premises Official Opening Ceremony Souvenir Magazine 1972 – 1979.

to research the setting-up of a driving centre. Road safety was a growing concern, and a driving school was part of the authorities' bid to professionalise the driving and riding industry and to raise safety standards. Before this, drivers and riders would take lessons from private instructors before registering for a test at various testing centres. Learners would get used to operating the machines in car parks and on quiet roads.

The Traffic Police asked if the SMCTA could organise a study trip to Japan as it had well-established riding schools, and the Traffic Police were keen to learn the Japanese system of testing. Robert arranged and led the 10-day trip. The Traffic Police sent three representatives, and the association sent three representatives – Robert, Mr Hoe Boon Meng of Hong Leong Corporation Ltd (distributor for Yamaha), and Mr Eng Seh Ping from Boon Siew (S) Pte Ltd (distributor for Honda). The group visited the Honda Rainbow testing centre, Yamaha testing centre, and Suzuki testing centre.

The Traffic Police eventually decided to work with Honda to set up a new driving school – the first of its kind in Singapore – called Singapore Safety Driving Centre (SSDC). The SSDC was to be established as a private joint venture between Japanese and Singapore parties to help raise riding standards among learner motorcyclists. Unlike other testing centres that tested riders on public roads, the SSDC would have its own circuit on which to test rider skills.

The authorities wanted SSDC to involve the players in the motor industry in order to secure their commitment to the success of this new venture. Partners included NTUC, which was a big motor insurance provider; Boon Siew, distributor of Honda in Singapore; Kah Motor, a major car distributor; Honda Rainbow Driving School of Japan; Honda Motor; and a private driving school. As a key player in the motorcycle industry, SMCTA was also invited to take up 5 per cent of the school's shares, which amounted to $100,000. This was a good investment opportunity but the SMCTA needed to raise funds in order to seize it.

Robert knew that it would be difficult to get dealers to contribute money, so he – together with a few committee members – came up with an innovative arrangement. There were five major motorcycle and scooter brands in Singapore – Yamaha, Honda, Suzuki, Kawasaki, and Piaggio. Each authorised dealer of each brand created a pool – for every bike the dealer sold, he would contribute $30, which would be collected by the distributor to ensure fairness and transparency.

As the association was not allowed to engage in business or commercial activities, a company called Singapore Motorcycle Industry Corporation (SMIC) was formed to collect the money. Once the targeted sum of $100,000 needed for the investment was achieved, the collection stopped. As the number of bikes sold at the time was about 1,000 units per month, it didn't take long to reach the target. SMIC used the $100,000 to take up 5 per cent of shares in the new driving centre in Ang Mo Kio. It then donated the shares to SMCTA, after which, SMIC was dissolved. Those shares in SSDC are worth $3 million today, and the SMCTA receives some $160,000 in dividends each year. This win-win arrangement ensured that the SMCTA and the trade benefitted without loss or disadvantage to anyone.

In the mid-1980s, the SMCTA had to help the motorcycle trade navigate one of its biggest crises as government moves to improve road safety led to new legislation that threatened to crush the industry.

Up to this point, most motorcycle riders held a provisional driving licence or "L" licence. This allowed them to ride, but they were not deemed fully qualified riders as they had not yet passed a final riding test. This provisional licence could be renewed every year for a small $10 fee. As a result, many riders simply renewed their L-licences repeatedly without ever bothering to sit for the final test to get their riding licence.

In August 1981, the government announced its intention to take L-riders off the roads[40]. Only in May 1984, however, did the authorities announce a hard deadline of 1 October 1985 to do so. This move was meant to improve road and rider safety as L-riders were found to be three-and-a-half times more likely to be killed in a road accident than a qualified rider[41].

Despite the government's announcement, many of the 95,000 L-riders were slow to act. Singapore's three testing centres could test about 540 riders a day but only half that number would show up. Of those who did register to take their riding tests, only one in five passed[42]. By August 1984, it was estimated that at this rate, only 18,900 L-riders would meet the deadline to get their licences.

This posed a severe threat to the industry and to the riders who depended on a motorcycle licence for their livelihood. The trade expected a 30 to 50 per cent drop in sales if the low pass rate continued. The SMCTA launched a $50,000 campaign to urge L-riders to take the riding test early[43]. When it appeared clear that getting the entire population of L-riders to pass the riding test by 1 October was going to be a huge challenge, the association organised a series of free training courses from 10 February 1985 until September that year to help riders familiarise themselves with the testing circuit and train for the obstacle course. It even brought in two Japanese riding instructors from Honda to set up the riding courses and to train 20 local instructors.

SMCTA's efforts went a long way in helping most of the L-riders to pass their tests and keep their bikes, even as some needed more than one attempt to clear the hurdle. But even so, the motorcycle trade was hit hard in 1985. In the lead-up to the 1 October deadline, motorcycle sales plummeted as buyers held off on buying motorcycles because of the impending change in the rules regarding L-riders. In that same year, Singapore suffered the worst depression it had seen yet[44], and this also hit sales hard. During the 1983 boom,

[40]   "Motorcycle sales hit 10-year low", *The Straits Times*, 30 September 1985, pp 11.

[41]   Ibid

[42]   "40,000 L-riders may 'lose' their m-cycles: Campaign opens to advise learners to take tests early", *The Straits Times*, 18 August 1984, pp 16

[43]   Ibid.

[44]   http://factsanddetails.com/southeast-asia/Singapore/sub5_7c/entry-3782.html#chapter-7

as many as 1,400 bikes and scooters were sold each month. In June 1985, only 490 were sold[45]. Some of the motorcycle dealers were in danger of going out of business.

Although motorcycle sales eventually picked up once the riding population and the motorcycle trade settled down and adapted to the new rules after 1 October, this body blow to the industry would have severe ripple effects. Competition, already fierce before the crisis, grew even more heated in the following years as traders fought to recover. The increasingly cutthroat competition among dealers would eventually force Ban Hock Hin to take a different tack.

In 1985, Robert decided to step down from the post of Honorary Secretary. He served one more term as the assistant to the Honorary Secretary to ensure a smooth handover to the newcomer. He then served as an adviser to the association and continues to do so today.

In appreciation of Robert's many years of service and commitment, the association presented him with a plaque in the traditional Chinese style bearing the Chinese words 领导有方 (ling dao you fang) meaning that Robert demonstrated effective leadership.

SMCTA presented this plaque to Robert in appreciation of his service and leadership at the association's 14th Anniversary celebrations in 1985 when Robert stepped down as the Honorary Secretary. He continues to serve as adviser to the association. The plaque now hangs over the main entrance to Ban Hock Hin.

---

45 "Motorcycle sales hit 10-year low", *The Straits Times*, 30 September 1985, pp 11

1980s: Shifting into High Gear

Out of the Ashes

In the first eight years after its 1971 incorporation as a private limited company, Ban Hock Hin flourished as the motorcycle industry continued to grow in tandem with Singapore's burgeoning economy.

The 1970s kept Robert busy as he laboured to build the trade association to represent the industry's interests and to coordinate effective responses to legislative and market changes. Ban Hock Hin was now doing very well – it was an authorised agent for all the major Japanese motorcycle brands in Singapore and was considered one of the three big players in industry. Its nett worth had multiplied from the $60,000 when Robert took over in 1971 to nearly $1 million in 1979. But a major crisis was about to strike.

On the last night of May 1979, Robert received a fateful phone call. Ban Hock Hin was burning, the caller said. Ah Yee, who had been living on the third floor, had gotten out of the building in time and was safe. But there was no saving the contents of the building.

Although shaken, Robert took the news calmly. The fire brigade was already there doing its job. There was little else he could do until the flames were put out. He got himself ready, climbed into his Mercedes Benz, and drove from Bukit Timah to Beach Road. By the time he arrived, the flames had been doused along with everything else in the shop. The front of the building was badly damaged, and the second and third floors were destroyed. San Chwee and Harry also came to survey the damage, but San Chwee was at a loss and left the clean-up to his eldest son. Harry disappeared at 11 a.m. that morning. Robert later found out that Harry had gone to Malaysia to gamble as he had originally planned.

Part of Robert's calm was knowing that fire insurance would compensate him for most of the losses. But there was still work to be done, and assets to be salvaged. Although the insurance pay-out would help cover losses from physical assets, there was one kind of asset that it didn't cover – assets such as crucial records, especially hire purchase records. Those documents represented hundreds of thousands, if not a million, dollars in hire purchase collection. As long as the records survived, the company – and hirers – would know how much remained to be paid and the contract between the two would stand. Without those records, there was no way the company could enforce the agreement.

Robert's move to transfer the hire purchase records from books to the Kardex system had proven fortuitous. The metal cabinet and trays that held the paper cards protected the information of more than 1,000 accounts. When hirers heard that Ban Hock Hin was in a fire – the blaze was reported on the front page of the Straits Times on 1 June 1979 – many called to gleefully ask how much remained on their hire purchase. The company's employees were able to retrieve the information and reply to them with confidence, much to the hirers' disappointment.

Although protected from the flames, those Kardex documents didn't move themselves. Robert remembers watching the accounts manager, Ms Fong Wai Ling, climbing precariously up and down a ladder to help salvage documents from the wrecked building. Long after the crisis had passed, he would continue to express admiration and gratitude for her and the other dedicated employees who helped the company through the tough days following the fire.

Customers were not the only stakeholders Robert had to reassure during that time. All the motorcycle distributors that Ban Hock Hin dealt with also paid the company a visit. Representatives from Boon Siew (Honda), Hong Leong (Yamaha) and Guan Hoe (Suzuki) came by the burnt site – they had all extended extensive credit to Ban Hock Hin, and some were worried that the fire had crippled Ban Hock Hin's ability to repay its debts. When they saw that all the hire purchase records had been safely retrieved and learned that insurance would cover the stock losses, they left relieved and reassured.

Salvage and retrieval were not the only priorities for Robert in the aftermath of the flames. He had to find a place for the business to operate out of. In the days immediately following the fire, Robert used San Chwee's property in Geylang as a temporary base of operations. San Chwee was already running his second-hand car business – Ban Hock Hin Motor Company – out of that site so it was a bit cramped for everyone for about half a year.

San Chwee's property in Geylang was sometimes used as a temporary store for Ban Hock Hin before the fire. After the incident, Ban Hock Hin moved its operations to Geylang while Robert looked for new premises. Circa 1976, before the fire at Beach Road.

Robert also managed to have the damage to the building at 131 Beach Road repaired in record time. On the very day of the fire, he took photos of the site and called the insurer's loss adjustors to come down to assess and log the damage. Once that was done, he engaged a contractor to clear the debris, patch the damaged roof, and paint the building. A week after the fire, the premises were ready for occupation.

However, Robert knew that he needed a new office location. In some ways, the business had already outgrown the old shophouse at 131 Beach Road. The aging building was cramped and had its limits; the electrical wiring was also old and faulty and had shorted, causing the blaze. More importantly, the fire had gutted the second floor, making it no longer safe to use. Their shop space was essentially halved. It was also rented. Although the row of shophouses was under a special rental control scheme that kept rentals very low, which was a good advantage, he knew that Ban Hock Hin needed a new home. Hence, he started looking for new premises.

Robert learned that one of his fellow members on the management committee of The Singapore Motorcycle Trade Association (SMCTA) planned to move out of a building at Rangoon Road. However, instead of taking over the rental, Robert negotiated with the landlord to buy over the building. The brown, three-storey building sat at the edge of Little India. It was a good location, fairly central, and easy for customers to get to. Robert ended up paying a book value of $500,000 for the building. The $200,000 pay-out from the insurance company helped to defray the costs while a loan from Tat Lee Bank took care of the balance.

In January 1980, Ban Hock Hin officially moved into 68 Rangoon Road. In another decade or so, Robert's decision would again prove to be a far-sighted one. The government acquired 131 Beach Road some years later. Although Ban Hock Hin was not the property owner, it was compensated $70,000 because it had occupied the space for some 50 odd years. If Ban Hock Hin had not moved the bulk of its operations to its own building in Rangoon Road, it would've been left homeless.

Ban Hock Hin's new home at 68 Rangoon Road.

But the move to Rangoon Road forced some critical changes on Ban Hock Hin, changes that would set it on a significantly different trajectory. Overheads increased greatly because of the building loan and because staff strength had doubled from six to 13 in order to operate two branches. Although the branch at Beach Road was well known because of its long history at that location, business after the fire slowed. Robert had to focus his energies on the Rangoon Road outlet, and without a skilled and motivated person to look after the business at Beach Road, it never quite recovered. However, the new Rangoon Road outlet needed time to build momentum and awareness in the market of its new location – even with Robert's full attention and support. He knew that for Ban Hock Hin to survive, it couldn't be business as usual.

Furthermore, he'd also realised that he couldn't count on his brother for help as Harry's heart was not in the business – on the day of the fire at Ban Hock Hin, Harry left for Malaysia to pursue his horse racing hobby before the sun was high. Robert had been left to steer the business through the crisis alone. Long before the fire, San Chwee had already told Robert that Ban Hock Hin needed him to survive. At this juncture, it seemed San Chwee's assessment was on the mark. Hence, Robert renewed his focus and efforts on building up the business.

Next, Robert had to find a different business model. At that time, motorcycle sales were concentrated in the hands of the authorised dealers for the motorcycle brands. Each sole distributor would appoint about 10 to 12 authorised dealers, usually the largest and most successful in the industry. Reputation and confidence were important commodities because the sole distributors would extend credit of one week to three months to their dealers. Smaller players in the market did not get credit terms, which limited their capacity to do business. As a result, many of them stuck to operating workshops and selling motorcycle accessories, which required less capital.

In addition, sole agents usually imposed a sales quota on its dealers, meaning that dealers had to commit to selling a certain number of motorcycles[46], which posed a business risk. It also led to fierce competition and undercutting practices among dealers. Profit margins on the sale of each bike were as low as $2. However, dealers could make a little more selling motorcycles on hire purchase (HP) and making money off the interest.

The vast majority of motorcycle buyers came from the lower income groups. Middle class buyers, however, were increasing fast, making up about 20 to 30 per cent at the start of the 1980s, up from 10 per cent in the past. The government's policies on car ownership was pushing even middle-income earners to turn to motorcycles. The two-wheelers were cheaper than cars and hire purchase (HP) schemes made motorcycles even more affordable. Down payment was usually 20 per cent of the machine's cost and the remaining amount was usually repaid over two years in monthly instalments. This new market segment meant that the motorcycle market still had opportunities and room to expand.

Robert then came up with a plan that could both help the smaller players get a foot in the market as well as broaden Ban Hock Hin's own distribution network and increase its sales volume. He developed a manual that gave specific details about the bike models in each brand, how much each cost, how much insurance cost, and how to calculate the HP down payment and monthly repayment sums over different repayment periods. He made it easy for anyone to do the calculations, and therefore, be able to sell motorcycles on hire purchase. He was even able to visualise and design the manual in such a way that made it easy for the user to find and understand the information he needed. Each manual had to be painstakingly typed up, its columns hand-drawn, and its pages hand-cut. This little black book became a sought-after asset in the industry, and dealers would approach Robert for a copy of the coveted manual.

46   "Bikes sellers fight to meet quotas", *New Nation*, 10 January 1980, pp4.

	RD125LC	RD250LC	RD350LC	XS400K	XZ550R	MODEL
	3,585	4,895	5,850	4,895	6,800	Nett Price
	15	19	35	40	69	Road Tax (6)
	5	5	5	5	5	Regn Fee
	20	20	20	20	20	No. Plate
	249	341	365	319	387	Comp P/Holder
	3,874	5,280	6,275	5,279	7,281	On the Road
	1,674	2,580	3,275	2,479	3,281	HP D/Payment
	2,200	2,700	3,000	2,800	4,000	LOAN
	119–20	146–00	162–50	151–70	216–60	24 Instalment
	100–85	123–75	137–50	128–35	183–35	30 Instalment
	–	108–75	120–85	112–80	161–10	36 Instalment
	3,585	4,895	5,850	4,895	6,800	List Price
	190	300	400	290	444	Dealer's Disc
	–	–	–	–	–	Add. Disc
	–	–	–	–	–	Incentive
	3,395	4,595	5,450	4,605	6,356	NETT PRICE
						Cost
	3,640	4,920	5,820	4,935	6,770	On the Road
	2,300	2,300	2,700	3,000	4,000	LOAN
	1,340	2,620	3,120	1,935	2,770	HP D/Payment
	124–60	124–60	146–25	162–50	216–60	24 Instalment
	105–40	105–40	123–75	137–50	183–35	30 Instalment

YAMAHA

A page from the manual on selling bikes on hire purchase. The pages were cut and typed up so that it was easy for the user to quickly access all the information he needed.

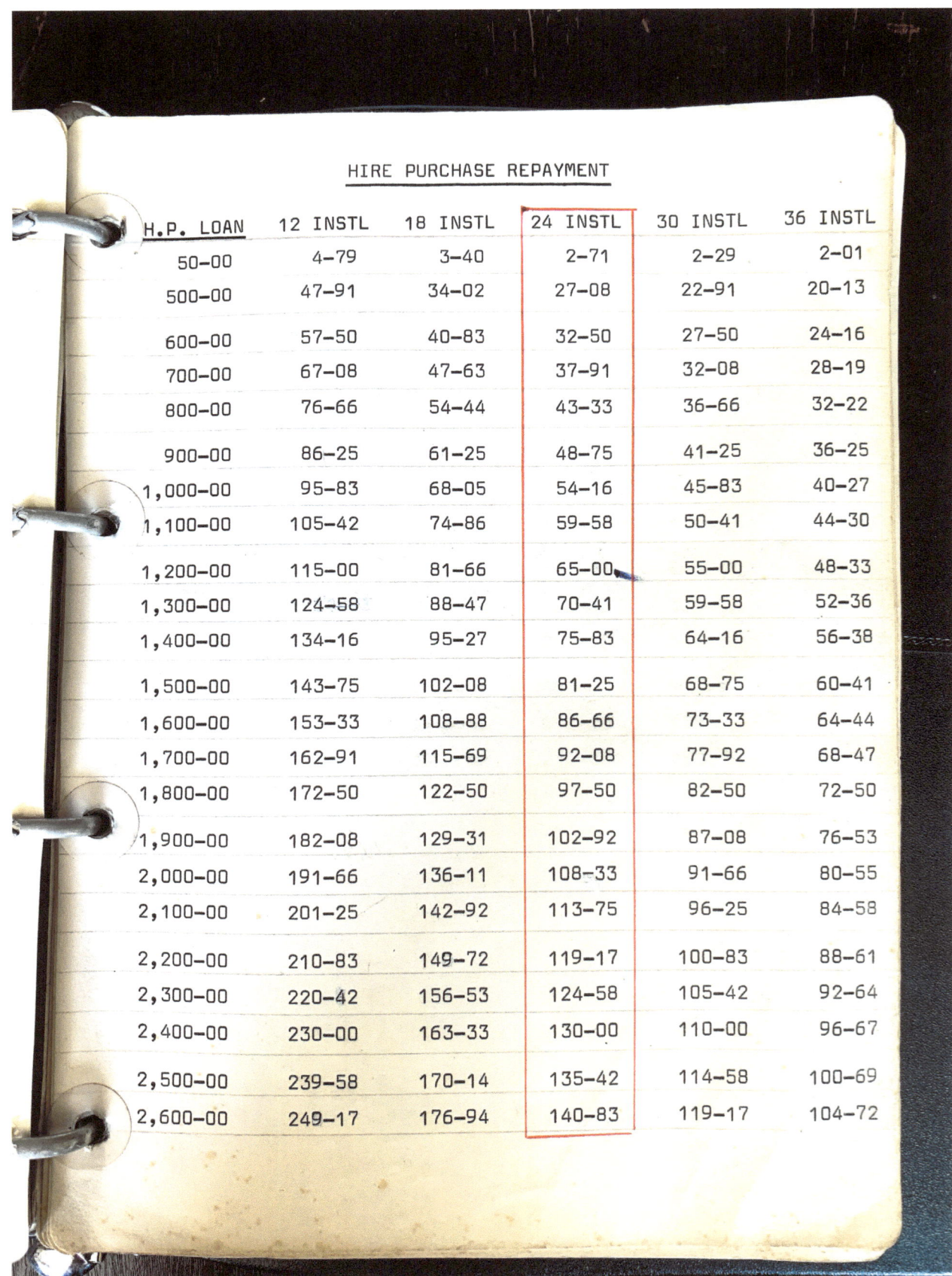

HIRE PURCHASE REPAYMENT

H.P. LOAN	12 INSTL	18 INSTL	24 INSTL	30 INSTL	36 INSTL
50-00	4-79	3-40	2-71	2-29	2-01
500-00	47-91	34-02	27-08	22-91	20-13
600-00	57-50	40-83	32-50	27-50	24-16
700-00	67-08	47-63	37-91	32-08	28-19
800-00	76-66	54-44	43-33	36-66	32-22
900-00	86-25	61-25	48-75	41-25	36-25
1,000-00	95-83	68-05	54-16	45-83	40-27
1,100-00	105-42	74-86	59-58	50-41	44-30
1,200-00	115-00	81-66	65-00	55-00	48-33
1,300-00	124-58	88-47	70-41	59-58	52-36
1,400-00	134-16	95-27	75-83	64-16	56-38
1,500-00	143-75	102-08	81-25	68-75	60-41
1,600-00	153-33	108-88	86-66	73-33	64-44
1,700-00	162-91	115-69	92-08	77-92	68-47
1,800-00	172-50	122-50	97-50	82-50	72-50
1,900-00	182-08	129-31	102-92	87-08	76-53
2,000-00	191-66	136-11	108-33	91-66	80-55
2,100-00	201-25	142-92	113-75	96-25	84-58
2,200-00	210-83	149-72	119-17	100-83	88-61
2,300-00	220-42	156-53	124-58	105-42	92-64
2,400-00	230-00	163-33	130-00	110-00	96-67
2,500-00	239-58	170-14	135-42	114-58	100-69
2,600-00	249-17	176-94	140-83	119-17	104-72

For any bikes that weren't already listed under the respective brands, manual users could refer to this table to easily determine the instalment sums based on the loan amount and repayment period.

NO.	COMPANY	TEL :	H	Y	K	S	V	B	SS
01	AUTEX TRADING CO	2934218/2934217	✓	✓		✓			
02	BAN HOCK HIN CO PTE LTD	2989122	✓	✓	✓	✓			
03	CHU SENG TAN KEE	3484900/3459368	✓	✓	✓	✓		✓	
04	ENG HUA TRADING CO	4522434			✓				
05	ENG KWONG MOTOR CO	7699564/2600312	✓						
06	HONG GUAN MOTOR (P) LTD	3360719/3377519 3383403	✓				✓		✓
07	HOCK SENG MOTOR (P) LTD	3372536/3361904			✓		✓		
08	HUP HIN	2709810						✓	
09	KATONG MOTOR	3480578					✓		✓
10	KHENG MOH (P) LTD	2982112	✓						
11	KIN SAI TRADING CO	3389638/3389630	✓	✓	✓	✓			
12	KIVILE ENT (P) LTD	2964590/2954593	✓	✓					
13	KOON SENG MOTOR	2206031					✓		✓
14	LEE HUAT MOTOR CO	7691717	✓				✓		✓
15	LEONG HIN CO (P) LTD	4405855/3443062			✓	✓			
16	LEONG LEONG MOTOR CO	2563290			✓				
17	LEONG SENG & CO	2737469			✓				
18	LIAN HUP BROS	7696655/2698831						✓	
19	MAH PTE LTD	2942704	✓	✓	✓	✓		✓	
20	MAH MOTOR AGENCY	2947648/2965456			✓			✓	
21	NEW UNION	4811059					✓	✓	
22	ORIENTAL MOTOR (P) LTD	4408116/3443837 7483128	✓	✓			✓	✓	

Robert kept detailed records of which dealers dealt in which brands.

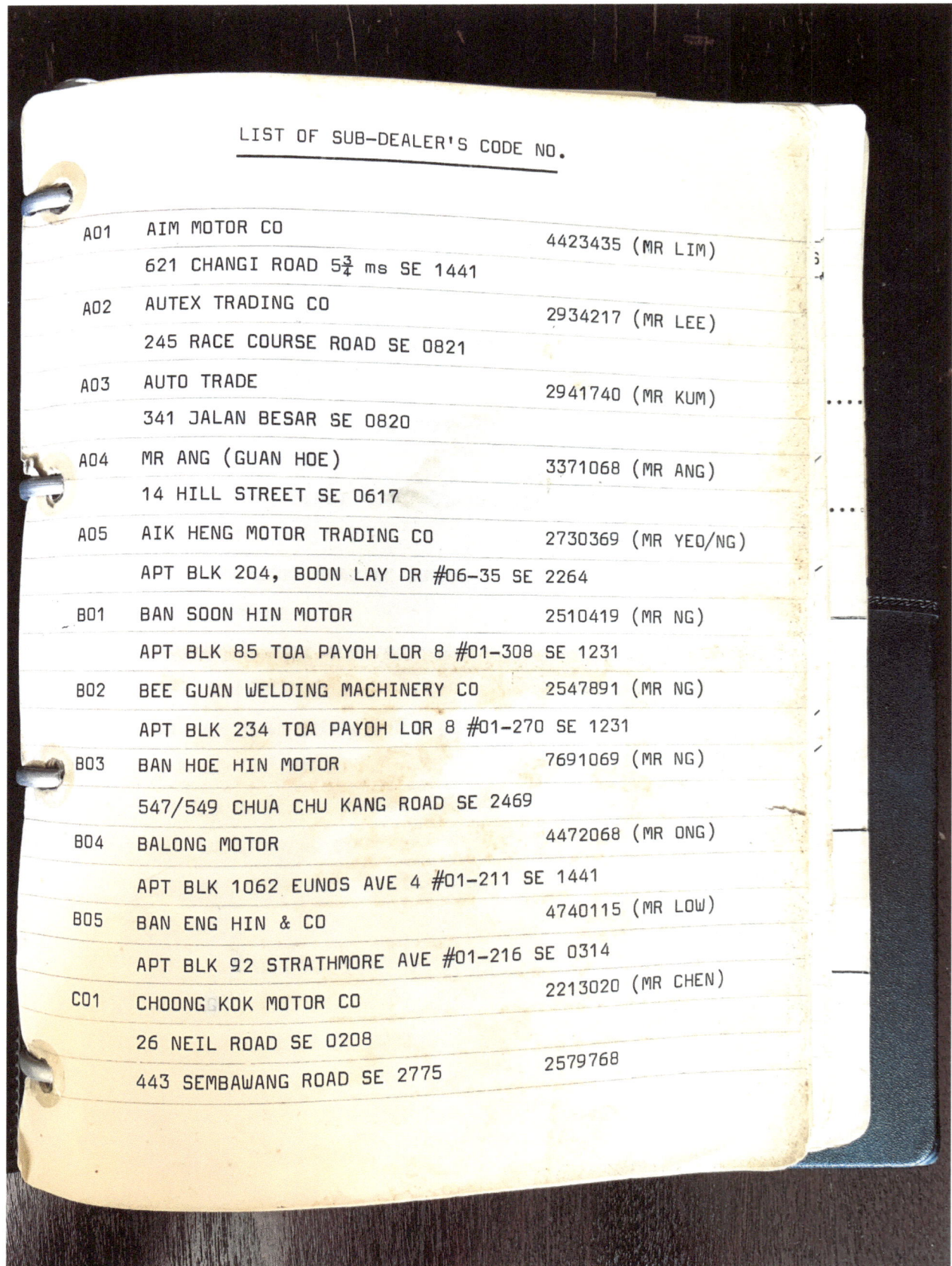

LIST OF SUB-DEALER'S CODE NO.

A01 AIM MOTOR CO   4423435 (MR LIM)
     621 CHANGI ROAD 5¾ ms SE 1441

A02 AUTEX TRADING CO   2934217 (MR LEE)
     245 RACE COURSE ROAD SE 0821

A03 AUTO TRADE   2941740 (MR KUM)
     341 JALAN BESAR SE 0820

A04 MR ANG (GUAN HOE)   3371068 (MR ANG)
     14 HILL STREET SE 0617

A05 AIK HENG MOTOR TRADING CO   2730369 (MR YEO/NG)
     APT BLK 204, BOON LAY DR #06-35 SE 2264

B01 BAN SOON HIN MOTOR   2510419 (MR NG)
     APT BLK 85 TOA PAYOH LOR 8 #01-308 SE 1231

B02 BEE GUAN WELDING MACHINERY CO   2547891 (MR NG)
     APT BLK 234 TOA PAYOH LOR 8 #01-270 SE 1231

B03 BAN HOE HIN MOTOR   7691069 (MR NG)
     547/549 CHUA CHU KANG ROAD SE 2469

B04 BALONG MOTOR   4472068 (MR ONG)
     APT BLK 1062 EUNOS AVE 4 #01-211 SE 1441

B05 BAN ENG HIN & CO   4740115 (MR LOW)
     APT BLK 92 STRATHMORE AVE #01-216 SE 0314

C01 CHOONG KOK MOTOR CO   2213020 (MR CHEN)
     26 NEIL ROAD SE 0208
     443 SEMBAWANG ROAD SE 2775   2579768

Robert's manual also had all the sub-dealers' information recorded neatly for him to refer to quickly and easily.

Additionally – and perhaps even more crucially – Robert gave the smaller dealers credit of two weeks, which was even longer than what some sole agents extended, so that they had the time to settle the financial arrangements with the customers. He also reduced smaller dealers' risk by not imposing a sales quota on them and even gave the dealers display bikes. When customers bought the bikes, they'd sign the hire purchase agreement and sales proposal form. The dealer would then pass the HP agreement to Ban Hock Hin, who would register the vehicle under the customer's name. When the registration was completed and a vehicle registration number was issued by the Registrar of Vehicles, Ban Hock Hin would install the number plate on the bike and deliver it to the dealer. Within two weeks, the dealer would have to pay Ban Hock Hin the down payment they had collected from the customer. Ban Hock Hin would then give the dealers $50 commission for each motorcycle they sold while charging them only $10 to do the registration, install the number plate, and even deliver the bikes.

On the surface, it looked like only the dealers benefited from this arrangement. Harry certainly couldn't understand what his older brother was doing with the business and had privately grumbled to others about the sub-dealer scheme. But Robert often thought – and calculated – far deeper than most. He wasn't eyeing the obvious profit that came from selling motorcycles; the real profit came from deftly managing credit terms and interest rates.

To recap, sole distributors would give Ban Hock Hin 90 days' interest-free credit. Ban Hock Hin would give the sub-dealers 14 days' credit. Hence, the company had 2.5 months of interest-free credit – or cash in hand – to use at its discretion. Ban Hock Hin, through the sub-dealers, would charge the customers or end users 13 to 15 per cent per annum on their hire purchase amount. With this arrangement, Robert built a network of 40 sub-dealers within six months of initiating it and was selling 400 bikes a month. At $3,000 a bike, this amounted to some $1.2 million in sales per month. In the 2.5 interest-free months, this amounted to some $3 million. Yet, interest charged to the customer started the moment they bought the bike. This meant that Ban Hock Hin could earn substantial amounts from interest alone. That profit could then be re-invested or used to increase the company's capital to finance more vehicles and generate even more revenue.

In reflection, Robert said the fire was a blessing in disguise, adding, "If a person doesn't face certain hardships, he may not have his best drawn out of him." The fire had converted the old motorcycle and spare parts stock the company held into cash via the insurance pay-out, which helped the business acquire the building at Rangoon Road. The new building and intensified business demands then forced Ban Hock Hin to expand in order to survive. In its own expansion, the business helped to build the industry. The forced expansion also led Ban Hock Hin to innovate and to adopt new technologies that came to lay critical foundations for its future transformation and survival. Not only did Ban Hock Hin weather the crisis caused by the fire, the company leapfrogged to a new level of operations and success in the 1980s because of it.

In an interesting parallel to his father's life, during the year that Robert was giving Ban Hock Hin a fresh start, of sorts, he welcomed the birth of his second son. This boy, born six days before Robert's 40th birthday, would one day continue the business that Robert had inherited from his father.

BAN HOCK HIN BUILDING

Ahead of His Time

Not long after Ban Hock Hin moved to Rangoon Road and the new sub-dealer distribution programme was in full swing, Robert watched a television programme in which then-Prime Minister Lee Kuan Yew talked about computers. The Singapore Government was vigorously promoting the use of computers, and the National Computer Board was going to be established on 1 September 1981 to promote, develop and expand the nascent computer industry in Singapore. Publicity about computers was widespread. Robert was reminded of his trip to Bridgestone Japan years ago and being told that computers could do the work of several people. It struck him that computers could be the solution to a growing problem at hand.

Thanks to Robert's sub-dealer programme, Ban Hock Hin now had a turnover of about $10 million a year and held a 25 per cent market share of all bikes sold in Singapore[47]. Staff strength had ballooned from six before the fire to 32 now. Selling 400 motorcycles a month – most of which are on hire purchase – meant that the number of Ban Hock Hin's HP accounts was multiplying fast, and the company had to keep detailed records of all of them. Physical records needed physical space for storage; they also needed many pairs of hands to search, manage, and update. Yet, good employees were hard to find and to keep, leading to a shortage of staff. A computer system would – could – solve many of those problems. However, computers were a relatively new idea at the time – at least its general use in most commercial entities was.

Computers had been around for some time, but they were mostly used by mathematicians, scientists, militaries, governments, and large business corporations. They were certainly not widespread, and the idea of a 'personal computer' had been introduced only in the late 1960s but hadn't quite taken off. Apple Computers and Microsoft had just been founded in the mid-1970s. The first IBM personal computer had just been introduced in 1981. Therefore, when Robert was thinking about incorporating information technology (IT) into Ban Hock Hin's operations in 1981, it was a somewhat radical idea – especially in the low-tech motorcycle industry. It was also expensive.

---

47   "From bicycles to computers", *New Nation*, 27 August 1981

Robert knew exactly what he wanted computers to do for the company, that is, improve his data collection, record, analysis, and management of the hire purchase department, insurance sales, and vehicle sales. He had a clear vision of how computers could transform the way the company operated. He saw that computerisation was the most effective way to produce the sorts of information he needed to make sound management and business decisions. Computers, with all that data collection and processing power, connected deeply with Robert's inherent need for information and order. However, as new as computers were to the market, there wasn't any off-the-shelf software that could meet Ban Hock Hin's needs. The only way that Robert could get the system he envisioned was if he were to customise it, which would drive the cost up even more.

But Robert never was one to let cost or convention get in the way of his vision. He engaged Far East Computers to put together his dream computer system for $90,000 (this figure eventually ballooned to $160,000) Each of the five terminals cost $6,000. The move was so gutsy that several newspapers wrote about Ban Hock Hin's plans to computerise when he first awarded the contract to Far East Computers. Making the bold decision and spending the money was the easy part; it would take Robert two painful years grappling with the software company before they could get the software designed to meet his expectations.

Far East Computers had assigned a systems analyst to study Ban Hock Hin's processes in order to design the software. He'd then show Robert the plans. However, designs on paper and functions in practice often didn't match up. The software designers didn't understand why Robert had so many requirements as the hire purchase and other systems appeared simple to outsiders. But Robert was looking ahead to the varieties of reports that he needed. He was trying to anticipate future needs whereas the designers were focused only on immediate operational demands. This difference in perspectives led to numerous heated exchanges and at one point, the computer company and its representatives, including its top management, stopped responding to Robert. As a last resort, Robert wrote a letter of complaint against Far East Computers to the new National Computer Board that had been formed to develop Singapore into a regional IT centre[48]. He copied that complaint to the managing director of Far East Computers. The next day, the managing director called Robert to mend fences, and from then on, Robert enjoyed the full cooperation of all staff of Far East Computers and the software could be completed according to his specifications.

When the computer system was ready, Robert hired 40 people to transfer the HP account data from the Kardex into the new system. He worked long hours and late nights for another two years to ensure that the new system worked properly. It would take him to the end of the decade before computers became fully integrated into company operations and the computer system stabilised.

Because the technology kept evolving, Robert had to repeatedly upgrade the operating system. Some of the IT staff of Far East Computers decided to break away and set up their

---

[48]   http://eresources.nlb.gov.sg/history/events/f499072d-330f-4763-a105-dd9940f1890b

own company, and Robert ended up working with them as they were cheaper and more willing to cooperate with their clients. By the start of the 1990s, computers had formed the backbone of the company's most essential functions, collecting data and producing the reports on which Robert based his management and business decisions.

He said: "Every minute of my time was worth it. If we had not gone through all that, our Integrated Business System will not be what it is today." At the time of writing, Ban Hock Hin's computer system – IBS – is one of, if not *the*, most sophisticated, flexible, and responsive in the motorcycle industry.

Computerising operations was no small task for this medium-sized company. Robert counts it as one of his biggest challenges and a significant milestone in the Ban Hock Hin's history. Not only did Robert find himself alone in his vision for the future, he had to put up with no small amount of derision from within and without. His own brother couldn't understand his single-minded drive to adopt this new-fangled technology. Ban Hock Hin had survived all this time without it; why should any expense and effort be spent on this unknown thing? Robert's peers were equally bemused. The motorcycle industry was a simple one – buy and sell. What was this fool's errand meant to prove?

At the time, Robert told a newspaper reporter: "Just because the old methods worked doesn't mean that there isn't a better way of getting things done. Medium-sized companies like ours have to put aside their old ways and automate for the future."[49]

Robert's foresight was not one that others easily understood, and yet, this bold move to computerise would set a crucial foundation for the next evolution of the company in the years to come.

This arduous experience also taught Robert a valuable lesson in management – for mission-critical functions such as IT, he could not afford to be left at the mercy of vendors and outsiders. He eventually hired his own IT specialist to continually develop the system in tandem with his persistent drive for improvement. This move proved to be a prescient decision when the time came for Ban Hock Hin to evolve yet again in the 1990s.

[49]   "Going on-line smooths way to efficiency", *Singapore Monitor* - 2nd edition, 5 September 1984, pp 2

Venturing Abroad

The mid-1980s brought new overseas opportunities for Ban Hock Hin. In 1985, Robert met a Vietnamese businessman called David Phan. David sourced products for Vietnam, which was deep in the throes of socialism. He represented a group of Montreal-based Vietnamese to source and send products back to Vietnam. The first order David gave to Robert was a tall one – 2,000 second-hand reconditioned Honda motorcycles to be delivered in three months. No other brand would do – the Vietnamese equated Honda to motorcycles and would accept no other brand. During the Vietnam War, Honda had supplied 6,000 motorcycles to the country. The Vietnamese thus grew accustomed only to Honda motorcycles. Furthermore, the bikes needed to arrive in Vietnam before 31 December or hefty taxes would kick in.

David's order was a first-of-its-kind job for the motorcycle trade in Singapore; no one here had done it before. But Robert was eager to enter the export market. By this time in 1985, the government's move to take riders with learner permits off the road was already hitting the industry hard. Local sales had slowed to a third of its normal levels. Export sales would be a critical new revenue stream.

Robert was thus determined to fulfil the order. He travelled to Japan to source used motorcycles from all over the country. Most of the models he could find were the Honda Cub 50 cc and 70 cc, with a number of 90 cc models mixed in. Then he travelled to Taiwan, which carried the cheapest Honda parts then, to source spare parts. Finally, he returned to Singapore to find someone to do the spray painting. He found a hardworking father and son duo.

Robert in Japan sourcing used motorcycles for recondition and export to Vietnam. He had to deliver 2,000 units in three months. Circa 1984.

One of the second-hand motorcycle yards Robert visited in Japan.

The Ban Hock Hin and spray-painting teams pulled late nights for weeks to meet the delivery deadline. Every machine had to be inspected and tested; its tyres, light bulbs and any other worn parts changed; and each had to be spray painted. The scale of the job was beyond the capacity of Ban Hock Hin's workshop at Rangoon Road. He sought help from a friend who let him use an empty lot of land that he had in Bukit Timah. The successful delivery of that order made the company a small mint – the staff that year received an 8-month bonus, the highest in the industry.

The Vietnamese group was so impressed with Robert's ability to deliver on such a challenging project that they continued to place large orders of second-hand bikes from Ban Hock Hin, although few orders were of such massive quantities. The group also invited Robert to Montreal, Canada, to see their operations and meet their key personnel. One of those key persons was Quah Tinh Van, or Van for short, who was a director of the group. They then proposed a joint venture with Robert.

Robert banded with some friends to set up Quan Ann Pte Ltd in 1986. Quan Ann then went into a joint venture with the Vietnamese to start the company Le Qun.

This venture gave Robert another valuable learning opportunity and opened his eyes to how international business worked. Le Qun secured the Yamaha sole distributorship for power products, such as outboard motors, generators, water pumps and spare parts. However, the Vietnamese market was a difficult one to penetrate. The market conditions in a developing economy with an uncertain political climate made doing business there tough. Robert found that the wartime hardships the locals endured fostered a business mindset that was at odds with his own. Market conditions were made harder when Vietnam suddenly decided to embrace capitalism through free-market reforms in 1986. The network and personal connections the Montreal group had in Vietnam also changed at that time and the business became unsustainable. In 1989, Robert and his partners decided to dissolve the company.

Independently of the Quan Ann venture, Ban Hock Hin continued exporting cars and bikes to Vietnam until the U.S. lifted sanctions on Vietnam in 1994. While sanctions were in place, business in the early 1990s was very lucrative. Ban Hock Hin would source decrepit machines from the U.S. and Japan and recondition them for export to Vietnam. After sanctions were lifted, however, U.S. and Japanese companies were able to deal directly with Vietnam, and middlemen like Ban Hock Hin were no longer needed.

During the latter half of the 1980s, Robert also gained valuable international experience doing business in another Southeast Asian country – Myanmar.

The 1980s was a turbulent time for Myanmar. The former British colony was deep in the throes of civil war, and the economy was at its nadir. On 3 November 1985, 25 per cent of the currency in circulation became worthless[50]; and in March 1987, the United Nations

---

50   Robert H Taylor, *The State in Myanmar*, NUS Press, 2009, p.377-378

declared Myanmar a Least Developed Country or LDC[51], a status reserved for the poorest and economically weakest nations in the world.

At the time, Robert had a Myanmar national called Yin Yin working for him. Through one of her contacts, Robert was introduced to a Myanmar businessman, U Aung Thoung, who wished to import motorcycles into Myanmar. Despite the economic troubles in Myanmar, Robert was intrigued. His business ventures in another developing Southeast Asian country – Vietnam – was paying off handsomely; could a venture to Myanmar? In 1986, he and some friends travelled to Yangon and to Mandalay to visit U Aung Thoung and find out.

Robert remembers the airport being very small, basic, and chaotic, like a 'village provision shop'. He stayed at the Inya Lake Hotel, which still stands today. When he turned on the tap, the water that flowed was 'black'. Electricity was intermittent – lights flickered on and off. The general levels of sanitation and hygiene shocked him. He remembers sitting at a food establishment and watching with some horror the grimy grey rag the server used to wipe his table. The server's threadbare singlet was the rag's twin. Yet, the food was very tasty and cheap; the seafood, very fresh.

The roads were crowded with trucks that served as buses – many were crammed with commuters, some of whom would hang precariously onto the rusty metal bars of the truck bed. Some of the trucks were so heavily laden in the rear that the front wheels of the vehicle would occasionally hover above the road. Robert shuddered looking at the perilous conditions. With so many such trucks plying the streets providing cheap transport to the masses, motorcycles were few.

The roads weren't all that held high risks. Business conditions weren't ideal either. The official exchange rate was US$1 to K6 (kyat); the black-market rate was US$1 to K250. Because the currency value was so unstable, it was popular practice to trade in gold, which could be used to exchange for paper currency. US dollars could be brought into Myanmar but could not be taken out – part of the government's stipulation that prohibited the outflow of foreign exchange. Investment laws also made business ventures difficult; connections were key, and on that front, U Aung Thoung had plenty. Besides, Myanmar had tremendous economic potential in the long run, and intrepid investors could also potentially benefit from getting involved at an early stage. Like some other foreign investors from Singapore, South Korea, Germany and other countries, Robert decided to give business in Myanmar a try.

In 1991, Ban Hock Hin went into a joint venture with government-backed Myanmar Economic Holdings Co (MEHC) with Aung Thoung as Ban Hock Hin's representative. A 1991 *Business Times* article reported that the joint venture – Ban Hock Hin Myanmar – had a paid-up capital of 10 million kyat or S$2.5 million. Robert appeared bemused at the figure. He remembers that Ban Hock Hin exported 50 units of new motorcycles to

---
[51]   *Ibid*, p. 379

Myanmar with an invoice of US$60,000 as its share in the company, nowhere close to the reported $2.5 million figure.

Ban Hock Hin went on to sell several shipments of motorcycles, cars, spare parts and even galvanised sheets to Myanmar. Profits from motorcycle sales were good but Robert couldn't take any of it out of the country. Many plans did not materialise because of inaction on the ground. Robert made about a dozen trips to the country over a course of about seven years. Eventually, though, the troubles of doing business in Myanmar outweighed the gains. Legal and auditing requirements and processes had become overly cumbersome. Ban Hock Hin Myanmar's activities tapered off and in 2002, the company was liquidated. It took another 17 years for the liquidation process to be completed. This experience stood in stark contrast to Ban Hock Hin's ventures in Vietnam and served as a valuable lesson in operating overseas.

Vietnam and Myanmar were not Ban Hock Hin's only overseas markets. The company also exported to Laos, Cambodia, Japan, Thailand, and the United Kingdom.

BAN HOCK HIN BUILDING

Filial Duties

The 1980s was a time of much grief and change for the Tan family. All of San Chwee and Kim Lian's children were married by this time and had children of their own. Harry had been widowed, having lost his wife to cancer, and was left to raise three young ones himself. The extended family would gather during Chinese New Year and for birthday parties, often at Robert's home at Toh Tuck Place where the children could run wild in the spacious garden of the corner terrace house. Several large casuarina trees lined the front of the garden by the main gate. The adults would sit beneath the gently swaying giants in the evening, sipping their drinks and enjoying the breeze. Those years of blissful extended family gatherings would be painfully few.

The extended Tan family at one of the gatherings at Robert's home at No. 1 Toh Tuck Place. Robert's wife, Alice (back row, fifth from the left, in glasses), was pregnant with their youngest child, Soon Cheong aka Rex. Circa 1979.

San Chwee had always enjoyed the good life; he indulged heavily in drink and food. His favourite food included braised fatty pork belly, mutton curry and roasted pig head. He liked fancy cars and stylish clothes – in his youth, he'd be decked out in a white suit. In his later years, he'd wear grey safari style shirts with a multitude of pockets. He never did care much for exercise. By the early 1980s he had wrapped up his car business in Geylang. He would sit at the Rangoon Road office, by the entrance, watching the comings and goings of the business with his thick, coke-bottle glasses nestled on his nose. As children, my brother Juice and I would visit the Rangoon Road office sometimes. 'Ah Kong' would always smile fondly at us and say things that we didn't understand. San Chwee spoke in a slurred and guttural manner, his words often sounding to me like rocks grinding against each other. I never could figure out what he was saying, nor what language he was saying it in. With his eyes hidden behind thick glass, I couldn't fully read his facial expressions either; he was an enigma to me.

San Chwee with two of his granddaughters – the author is on the right, and her cousin, Denyse (Su En), is in San Chwee's arms. Circa 1978.

San Chwee remembered his father fondly, or at least with much filial piety. Each year at Qing Ming or All Souls' Day, he'd labour up the slopes of Bukit Brown Cemetery, heaving himself up the steep inclines and navigating around the many graves, to pay his respects to his father, Kow Sai. He would bring with him an entire roasted pig head, slabs of roast pork, a whole steamed chicken, deep-fried whole fish, bags of fruit, hard liquor, and large quantities of paper offerings. After Kim Lian converted to Christianity, she wanted no part of this ancestral practice, but San Chwee carried on. He would bring Robert and his nephew Ah Hock with him until his declining health and poor mobility in the early 1980s forced him to stop. To this day, Robert honours this practice every year with his extended family. It has become one of the clan's favourite occasions to gather. Although we no longer haul a roasted pig head up the cemetery slopes on the inevitably muggy mornings we visit the grave, we always bring along a bottle of Hennessy XO. I'm sure ancestor Kow Sai enjoys brandy for breakfast nearly as much as we do.

San Chwee was religious about observing the Qing Ming festival, or All Soul's Day. Each year he'd bring lots of food and drink up the slopes of Bukit Brown cemetery to offer to his father, Kow Sai. You can see the red pig's head and a bottle of liquor in front of Kow Sai's headstone. Here, San Chwee (middle) was accompanied by Robert (far right); Robert's wife, Alice (far left); and Robert's eldest son, Eng Joo or Juice. Alice was pregnant with her youngest son, Soon Cheong, in this picture. Circa March 1979.

The grave of Tan Shen Heung aka Kow Sai in Bukit Brown cemetery. The family continues to observe Qing Ming every year. It is one of our favourite times to get together. The roasted pig's head has been replaced by a braised duck. Robert's wife, Alice, has taken over the preparation of food and paper offerings. Circa 2016.

Robert, his siblings and their children continue San Chwee's practice of paying respects to Kow Sai during Qing Ming each year. From left to right: Alice, Chin Bee (Diane), Denyse, Cheng Bee, Eileen, Bee Bee, Kay Kian, Kay Tuck, and Robert. 2016.

In the middle of September 1983, 63-year-old San Chwee suffered a devastating stroke. He was rushed to hospital, but he was incapacitated and couldn't move or speak. Kim Lian, as an extremely devout Christianity, set out to convert her husband and brought a preacher to see him at the hospital. San Chwee had never shown much interest in religion and had given only a cursory nod to Taoist practices. But as he lay immobile on the thin bed in the open-air ward at Singapore General Hospital, the preacher held San Chwee's hand and told him to squeeze it if he wanted to convert to Christianity. Bee Bee remembers watching the scene as the preacher suddenly exclaimed that San Chwee had squeezed his hand!

Kim Lian pronounced her husband saved in the eyes of the Lord and insisted on a Christian burial when he died on 17 September. But Robert had only ever known his father to subscribe to Taoist ideas, even if he wasn't particularly devout. He couldn't accept that his father would suddenly turn to a foreign religion. Kim Lian eventually got her way, and San Chwee's obituary acknowledged him as a follower of the Christian faith. But the battle over the obituary was not yet done.

San Chwee had four other common-law wives. One of them, Kim Hiok or Gold Leaf, had run off in the 1970s, taking their son, Siew Chuan, with her. No one has heard from her since. Kim Lian wanted the rest of the common-law wives – and their children – struck from the obituary. But Robert objected. He reasoned that the funeral rites, including the obituary, should unapologetically reflect San Chwee's life and what he would've wanted. However, by Kim Lian's reasoning, she was the only legitimate wife. In the end, Robert won out. All of San Chwee's women and children were listed in the obituary, save for Kim Hiok and her son.

Once the funeral rites – held at the Geylang home – were completed and San Chwee's body was cremated and the ashes interred at the Mandai Columbarium, attention turned to legal matters.

San Chwee didn't leave a will. He didn't hold many assets but the significant one he did own was 33 per cent of Ban Hock Hin's shares. According to inheritance law, 50 per cent of those shares went to the four wives, and the remaining 50 were distributed among the children. Each child's share was worth $6,945.

As the eldest son, Robert felt it was his duty to uphold his father's honour and fulfil his responsibilities. When San Chwee lived, he gave each of his wives a monthly allowance. Upon San Chwee's death, his wives no longer had any financial support. As Kim Lian was his mother, Robert gave her $1,400 each month from his personal funds until she died. Robert had always felt deeply for Ah Yee; he reminded the family often that Ah Yee was the one who cared for and essentially raised most of Kim Lian's children. Robert thus gave $600 from his own funds to Ah Yee each month until she passed away in the 2000s.

This left the other two wives – Ah Huey and Mary – with whom Robert had no personal relationship or connection. Yet, his sense of duty and compassion demanded that he not leave them in a lurch. He knew that legal procedures would take time to complete, which meant that any inheritance the two women and their children had would not be released to them for a time. But they had bills to pay and needed to eat. Hence, he continued to give each of them nearly a $1,000 every month, but this sum was borrowed against the Ban Hock Hin shares that they'd inherit. When their inheritance was finally released to them, they'd have to pay back in the number of shares they had borrowed against. Robert also paid the school fees of his half-siblings who were still completing their studies.

Three years later, in 1986, more trouble came knocking. By then, Harry's gambling habit had driven him into debt. He asked Robert to use Ban Hock Hin funds to help him pay what he owed; Robert said no. Not only was this against his long-standing principle of keeping personal and company funds separate, Ban Hock Hin's cash was also tied up financing the sub-dealer network and hire purchase scheme.

Desperate, Harry asked Robert to buy over his shares in Ban Hock Hin so he could settle his debt.

Robert contemplated his options. A part of him was done working with Harry. His younger brother's approach to life and business sorely conflicted with his own. Harry's willingness to abandon the business – and him – during the company's worst crisis in 1979 also caused Robert to doubt his brother's commitment to the business. And now Harry's personal problems were starting to encroach on Ban Hock Hin's interests.

At this time, Robert and some business partners had recently set up the import-export firm, Quan Ann. Even before Harry's debt crisis surfaced, Robert had already been thinking of leaving Ban Hock Hin to Harry's devices and striking it out on his own at Quan Ann. At this juncture, however, he decided to give Ban Hock Hin a last shot.

Robert called for a meeting of all Tan family members who held Ban Hock Hin shares. He explained Harry's situation to all and asked if any of them wanted to buy Harry's shares. Anyone who was keen to run the family business was free to step up now. No one took up the offer. Robert then asked if anyone wanted to sell him their shares – if he was going to buy over Harry's shares, he might as well buy over the shares of anyone who was inclined to sell. Ban Hock Hin shares were of no real value to anyone unless the company was sold or liquidated. By selling their shares, the family members could turn those assets into cash. Everyone chose to sell their shares to Robert.

Robert needed cash to buy out everyone. He borrowed money from Quan Ann in order to pay off all his siblings and San Chwee's widows. Then, Robert sold his property at Toh Tuck Place to raise the funds to pay back Quan Ann. He had bought the corner terrace for $120,000 in 1977. When he had to sell it in 1986, Singapore was just recovering from its worst recession in 1985, and housing prices remained depressed. Even so, he managed to sell it for $450,000.

Once Harry paid his creditors, he thought to continue working at Ban Hock Hin, but Robert would have none of that. Robert now wanted full control of his own fate – and that of the company he'd gone to so much trouble to save. Robert and Harry parted ways.

Toward the end of the 1980s, Robert decided to rope his youngest brother, Richard, into the business. Given Ban Hock Hin's growth on multiple fronts, Robert needed more support. Richard was living in Sydney, Australia. Although an engineer by training, he was managing a gas station in a partnership with several friends, which didn't seem to put his technical know-how to much use. Robert paid Richard a visit in Australia and suggested Richard return to Singapore to help him with the business. His technical knowledge and skills would be an important asset to the company. Richard agreed and moved his family back to Singapore in 1989. As Robert had foreseen, Richard's technical skills did become important in helping Ban Hock Hin seize interesting business opportunities in the next two decades.

1990s: The Big Switch

Taking Time Out

The 1990s opened with a personal tragedy for Robert.

One of his best friends took his life in Robert's apartment on Fort Road in 1990. His friend was a successful banker but came under investigation. Although innocent, the investigations triggered extreme anxiety in his friend. One February morning, Robert's friend died by suicide.

His friend's sudden, violent death shook Robert deeply. He'd lost his best friend in the worst possible way, and the days that followed were dark for Robert. He took his family to the Maldives on a quiet beach vacation and tried to deal with the shock and grief. But such a trauma is not an easy thing to shrug off.

That year, he decided to lighten his involvement in the business and semi-retire. He handed the management of daily operations of Ban Hock Hin to Richard, his youngest brother. Robert then took up golf. He had bought a membership at Sembawang Country Club years ago on a tip that the country club, although largely for military personnel, had a small quota for civilians and that quota was not filled. He bought the membership in 1972 for $2,000. Now that he wanted to retire, he thought golf seemed a suitable retirement type sport, especially since he already had a golf membership.

In classic Robert style, he threw himself into his new hobby. He took lessons, watched videos, and spent long hours at the driving range. Golf would come to fascinate him for decades – it was one thing he could not easily master. He would experiment with his swing and tweak a dozen parts of the swing a million times. He would also pick up a few more golf memberships along the way, trying out the different courses, fully immersing himself in the game. Overseas holidays became golfing holidays. Robert even set out golfing challenges – one of his favourites was to play three rounds of golf in a single day. Night golf at Orchid Country Club made that possible. Even on the days he played two 18-hole rounds of golf, he'd head to the driving range right after to continue working on his swing, hundreds of balls at a time.

Robert's approach to golf reflected his approach to achieving all his goals. He often said that to succeed, you need 信心 (xin xing)·决心 (jue xing)·耐心 (nai xing) – confidence in oneself, determination to achieve one's goals, and patience to wait for the results. Thirty years after picking up golf, his self-assuredness that he would one day master the game had not waned. Neither had his painstaking daily efforts to improve his skill, nor his long wait to achieve single handicap status.

After taking a two-year sabbatical, Robert bounced back with vigour. And just in time, too. Ban Hock Hin was about to embark on a war for scooter supremacy.

Fighting Scooter Wars

In Singapore, the East Asiatic Co (EAC) had been distributing Piaggio scooters since the 1960s[52]. Robert recalls it to be a conservative company that represented many types of products. In the hyper-competitive motorcycle and scooter market of the late 1980s and early 1990s, the Japanese brands were very aggressive, but EAC was seen to be less so. It was also less willing to take commercial risks, it seemed.

Piaggio's overseas sales manager, Mr Fornecheli, was in Singapore on business in 1990 and happened to meet Robert at an SMCTA meeting. He learned that Ban Hock Hin had been distributing the India-made LML Vespa since 1987, but even with an inferior and less well-known product, Ban Hock Hin was able to go head-to-head with the well-established Piaggio brand in the Singapore market. Mr Fornecheli was curious as to how this could have been done.

He later approached Robert with a business proposition. Piaggio had a new type of scooter, one with a plastic body instead of metal, called the Sfera. Although it had a stylish design, it was a smaller capacity model – just 80 cc. Most bikes in the market already were a minimum of 125 cc. Piaggio had been trying to get EAC to launch this new generation scooter for three years but EAC was resistant, saying that nothing under 100 cc will sell in the Singapore market. Piaggio offered Ban Hock Hin a non-exclusive distributorship if it would carry and promote the Sfera.

Robert agreed to consider the proposition. He ordered (and paid for) two units of Sfera 80 to test and found the scooter to have a powerful pickup despite the small capacity engine. The plastic body was light and unique, and the design, elegant and stylish. It also came in attractive, eye-catching colours. Robert decided to give it a shot. He ordered a small shipment and Ban Hock Hin was awarded the Piaggio distributorship in December 1991. Piaggio didn't cancel EAC's distributorship, though. Instead, Piaggio used Ban Hock Hin's involvement to pressure EAC into launching the Sfera as well.

---

[52] Christopher Tan, "Comfort clinches franchise for Piaggio scooters", *Business Times*, 15 October 1996, p.1

It probably didn't help matters that Ban Hock Hin and EAC weren't on friendly terms to begin with. In the 1960s, EAC had appointed Ban Hock Hin as an authorised dealer for Piaggio. However, the relationship soured under San Chwee's indelicate care, and subsequently, EAC refused to have anything further to do with the local company even after Robert took over and turned things around for Ban Hock Hin.

Now that Ban Hock Hin had nicked EAC's sole distributor status, the relationship soured even more. Ban Hock Hin aggressively advertised and promoted the Sfera and later, other new Piaggio models such as the 125 cc Skipper and wildly popular 150 cc Hexagon. It offered highly attractive hire purchase terms to customers – up to four years instead of the usual two. Buyers could ride away with the $4,000 Sfera for a mere $450 downpayment and monthly instalments of as low as $110. Ban Hock Hin even set up a showroom at River Valley Road to showcase the Piaggio scooters. The competition between the two distributors heated up in the first half of the 1990s although Ban Hock Hin was by far the more aggressive of the two when it came to marketing and promotions.

The showroom that Ban Hock Hin set up to showcase Piaggio bikes.

For example, Ban Hock Hin sponsored and helped organise a bikers' charity ride and carnival on 15 May 1994 to raise funds for the Community Chest. Some 600 bikers took part in a 10-km charity ride, called Bikers with a Heart, from Dempsey to the National Stadium. Then-Minister for Communications and the Environment Mah Bow Tan was the guest-of-honour.

The banner bearing Ban Hock Hin's and Piaggio's logo. Some 600 bikers took part in the 1994 charity ride which ended at the National Stadium. The event raised funds for Community Chest.

Ban Hock Hin sponsored four Skipper scooters that were then designed by sports stars Fandi Ahmad (soccer), Abbas Saad (soccer), Grace Young (bowling), and actress Aileen Tan. The scooters were auctioned, raising $31,500 for the Community Chest.

From left to right: Fandi Ahmad, Grace Young and Abbas Saad. The sports stars are seen here posing with the Skippers that they designed for auction at the Bikers' Charity Carnival in 1994.

The following year, Ban Hock Hin donated $20,000 to another community event for bikers. The first Custom Bike Competition was organised by grassroots organisations in Tampines North to foster closer relationships with riders and policy makers[53]. Ban Hock Hin also provided the new Piaggio Hexagon for the guest-of-honour Mr Mah to ride at the event.

---

[53] Ida Bachtiar, "Three-day carnival to bring bikers, authorities closer", *The Straits Times*. 18 Jnuary 1995, pp 3.

Robert (far right) presenting a cheque for Ban Hock Hin's donation of $20,000 to the 1995 Bikers' with a Heart event. Then-Minister for Communications and the Environment Mah Bow Tan (centre) was the guest-of-honour.

The new models' modern designs and the distributors' marketing efforts drove Piaggio sales to the highest they had been since Vespa's heyday in the 1950s. Furthermore, a new scooter customer profile emerged – that of young riders who loved the stylish vibe of the new-generation Piaggios. The scooters also found favour with female riders, who found the automatic transmission easier to operate and the lighter plastic bodies easier to handle[54]. Sales were helped by rising Certificate of Entitlement (COE) prices for cars, which drove some motorists to opt for economical two-wheelers instead. SMCTA records showed that Piaggio scooters went from a 6.8 per cent share of the two-wheeler market in 1988 to over 40 per cent in 1994[55]. The rejuvenated two-wheeler market hit a nine-year population high of 124,647 in November 1994[56].

Meanwhile, EAC largely just sat back and enjoyed the renewed interest in Piaggio scooters. It rode on its established reputation as the Piaggio distributor and reaped the rewards of Ban Hock Hin's marketing and advertising efforts. It did make some effort to assert its position as the incumbent distributor, however. For example, EAC dangled the chance to win free trips to Australia's Gold Coast and Malaysia' Langkawi for those who bought a Piaggio bearing an EAC badge.

---

[54] Ida Bachtiar, "Scooters ride up sales charts again", *The Straits Times*, 4 December 1994, pp 2.

[55] Ibid.

[56] Leong Ching Ching, "Motorcycles on the road hit a nine-year high", *The Straits Times*, pp 3.

Robert and his team were deeply displeased that EAC appeared to be freeloading off their intensive efforts and complained to Piaggio. This kind of arrangement was unfair to Ban Hock Hin. But Piaggio remained indecisive.

On the surface, Ban Hock Hin's business in 1994 was good. It sold twice as many vehicles in October and November that year compared to the same period in the previous year[57]. The export business to Asia and to Europe during the early 1990s was also in high gear. In addition to the large numbers of vehicles that Ban Hock Hin exported to Vietnam, it also did roaring business exporting big bikes to Japan and to Europe. Annual revenue exceeded $40 million[58].

However, Robert was soon alerted to a looming crisis. His accounting department had been faithfully collecting and presenting financial data, which Robert had previously called the 'eyes' of the business so one can see where one is going. This data now showed Robert that the company was headed to possible financial disaster.

The war with EAC was a costly one. In Ban Hock Hin's determination to promote sales, it had adopted a risky strategy – that of requiring low down payment and extending the hire purchase repayment period to four years. Although this move was hugely successful in generating sales, it created a cash flow problem for the company.

A large portion of the hire purchase was blocked – or outsourced – to finance companies, which extended only 18-month repayment period to Ban Hock Hin, as was the typical practice. Ban Hock Hin, however, extended 48 months to customers. In other words, Ban Hock Hin's collections fell far short of what it needed to repay the finance companies. Although it was earning high revenue, the volume of business meant that a lot of cash was tied up in its trade activities. If things remained unchanged, Ban Hock Hin would eventually run out of cash. If a company defaulted on even a single bank payment, it could do irretrievable damage to its reputation. In Robert's mind, the very survival of Ban Hock Hin was at stake.

The situation was bad enough that Robert felt he needed to warn his family. He gathered his wife and children in a family meeting to explain the financial position of the company. Although the problem was daunting, he didn't give up on finding solutions.

First, he ended the 48-month hire purchase scheme. Then, he came up with a plan to get the company back on a solid financial footing, but it required help from a bank. With a sound plan in hand, Robert was able to secure a bridging loan of $2 million from Bank of China to help the company tide over its cash flow problems. Robert's financial prudence over the years had helped Ban Hock Hin transform its tattered financial reputation under San Chwee's watch into one that ensured it could secure large bank loans to see it through tough times. Hence, the financial crisis could be averted.

Despite the extent of Ban Hock Hin's commitment to promoting Piaggio, the Italian

[57] Leong Ching Ching, "Motorcycles on the road hit a nine-year high", *The Straits Times*, pp 3.
[58] Christopher Tan, "On the comeback trail", *Business Times*, 11 May 2000, pp 26

principal stubbornly refused to make either Ban Hock Hin or EAC sole distributor of the brand. Piaggio was caught in a bind. The Italian company had a long-standing relationship with EAC, not just in Singapore but also in Italy. By this time, Piaggio had also gone into business with Ban Hock Hin in Vietnam and couldn't afford to jeopardise its operations there by choosing EAC over Ban Hock Hin in Singapore.

Robert was disappointed that his commitment to Piaggio had not been reciprocated with a sole distributorship. He also felt increasingly frustrated by Piaggio's indecision as having two competing distributors in a small market such as Singapore was not sustainable. He felt that EAC was unfairly benefiting from Ban Hock Hin's aggressive promotion of Piaggio. He'd even had to dodge a financial bullet in his efforts to make the brand a success. As a result, Robert decided to give up the distributorship and focus his energies elsewhere.

One of Ban Hock Hin's former executive directors, Yeo Eng Seng, had heard that Comfort Group was looking to enter the vehicle distributing market. The transportation group already operated some 10,000 taxis and was keen to expand its business and had been acquiring a number of car franchises[59]. Eng Seng then helped to broker a deal between Comfort and Piaggio with Robert's blessings. Robert knew that if Ban Hock Hin gave up the Piaggio distributorship, EAC would never agree to deal with Ban Hock Hin, thereby cutting off its source of Piaggio machines. If a third party like Comfort got the franchise instead – and Ban Hock Hin and Comfort were already collaborating in Vietnam – Ban Hock Hin could continue to sell Piaggio bikes as a dealer.

News of the change in franchisee broke in the *Business Times* on 15 October 1996. Despite the article reporting that both EAC and Ban Hock Hin appeared unaware of the impending change, Robert and Richard said they not only were aware of move, they strongly encouraged it. Nevertheless, future newspaper reports would maintain the impression that Ban Hock Hin had 'lost' the distributorship to Comfort[60].

In 1998 and in 2000, Ban Hock Hin went on to represent China-made Elite electric bicycles and Italian scooter brand, Italjet, respectively. It also snagged the distributorship for the uniquely designed Benelli Adiva bikes that come with a roof. Although these brands enjoyed brisk sales, Robert knew that the company needed to evolve its business strategy in order to survive. Moving products alone was not going to a sustainable approach for growth.

Tough times also dogged the motorcycle trade, which was buffeted by both economic factors as well as changes in government regulations.

Back in October 1991, the Singapore government imposed new emission standards for motorcycles. Japanese models made up the vast majority of two-wheelers sold in Singapore, and unfortunately, many of these models didn't meet the new standards.

---

[59]   Christopher Tan, "Comfort clinches franchise for Piaggio scooters", *Business Times*, 15 October 1996, pp 1.

[60]   Christopher Tan, "On the comeback trail", *Business Times*, 11 May 2000, pp 26.

Despite the popularity of Japanese bikes here, Singapore remained a small market to Japanese bike makers. Therefore, they were less eager to tweak their bike designs and production set-ups just to meet this market's needs. They could eventually ship vehicles that were compliant to the new standards, but it would take time. This left only 50 models on the market that complied with the new standards when they were introduced. This caused a near standstill in motorcycle sales. It also caused a huge problem for dealers who were still holding stock of vehicles that could no longer be registered. The timely introduction in 1992 and 1993 of the new Piaggio scooter models – which did meet the new emission standards – therefore helped boost two-wheeler sales.

As the popularity of the new Piaggio models grew and the introduction of new two-wheeler models that complied with the new emission standards helped bring buyers back to the market[61], vehicle sales started to recover. But just as the two-wheeler population hit a nine-year high in 1994, the government made another move that crippled it. The slump in sales following the introduction of new emission standards contributed to an excess of 5,157 'unused' motorcycle COEs from 1992 to 1993. In 1994, the Government suddenly reallocated these 5,157 COEs to the car categories. This move caused a severe shortage of COEs relative to demand from a rejuvenated two-wheeler market and drove motorcycle COE prices up from $1 in 1993 to $2,002 in December 1994[62]. This ended the age of $1 motorcycle COEs, and thereafter, motorcycle COEs would see one shocking premium record after another. In March 2017, motorcycle premiums hit $8,081 – more than the cost of most Class A (under 200 cc) motorcycles.

The 1994 reallocation of motorcycle COEs to car categories was merely a link in a long chain of events that buffeted the motorcycle industry. It added to the devastating effects of the authorities' move to take L-licences off the roads in 1985 and the introduction of new emissions standards in 1991. Furthermore, in 1996, the authorities raised the minimum riding age from 16 to 18, which also had a significant effect on bike sales as these new riders made up a significant proportion of bike buyers. To survive, dealers kept undercutting each other, driving Hire Purchase (HP) interest rates to new lows. In the latter half of the 1990s, HP interest rates in the motorcycle industry slid from a high of 15 per cent per annum in the early 1980s to a mere 2 or 3 per cent per annum.

Yet, the rate of delinquency – or failure of hirers to repay their loans – climbed to some 12 to 14 per cent. In other words, profits dived while risks skyrocketed. Given Ban Hock Hin's scale of operations and accompanying overheads, it couldn't survive on slivers of profit like the smaller dealers could. Robert had to find another way since motorcycle retail sales were an increasingly unattractive business. Even Comfort Group, which took over the Piaggio distributorship in 1995, gave up on the franchise by 1999 "after failing to stem losses from Day One"[63]. Piaggio would eventually come to represent its own brand in the Singapore market.

---

[61]   Leong Chan Teik, "Motorcycle COE price soars to all-time high of $1,802", *The Straits Times*, pp 21.

[62]   Ibid.

[63]   Christopher Tan, "Comfort gives up Peugeot, Piaggio distributorships", *Business Times*, 18 November 1999, pp 4

Scaling Up

Robert noticed that many organisations owned large motorcycle fleets. These included the Singapore Armed Forces, Singapore Traffic Police, Singapore Civil Defence Force, and Singapore Post Limited. Smaller fleet owners included commercial entities that used motorcycles for servicing and delivery activities. These fleet owners were no strangers to Ban Hock Hin. In the 1970s, Robert played a part in convincing the government to switch from using British bikes for the traffic police fleet to Japanese ones. At the time, Ban Hock Hin was already supplying and repairing bikes for government agencies such as the Public Works Department (PWD). The PWD was also the procurement arm for many government agencies then.

When the Traffic Police needed to replace their bikes, PWD asked Robert for his advice on bike model options. The Traffic Police had been using British Norton bikes, but spare parts were difficult to get. Robert recommended that the authorities consider using Japanese brands, such as Honda. The Japanese models performed well and were priced reasonably. Their brands and distributors also kept ample stock of spare parts and provided technical support.

When PWD called for the tender, Ban Hock Hin bid for the contract using the Honda 450P and won it. By July 1973, the entire Enforcement Squad of the Registrar of Vehicles used the Honda 450P. The Mobile Squad of the Traffic Police had 30 units with another 55 units on order[64]. The Traffic Police later bought even bigger capacity bikes like the 750 cc Honda[65] and 1100 cc Yamaha[66] bikes to tackle the hell rider scourge of the late 1970s. The company also vied for and won military tenders. Ban Hock Hin would go on to win numerous government contracts over the years and fulfil them successfully.

[64]   "Now the Hondas make more inroads here", *New Nation*, 16 July 1973, pp 9.

[65]   "Mobile Squad to get more speed", *The Straits Times*, 10 December 1977, pp 21.

[66]   Mobile Squad's answer to hell riders", *The Straits Times*, 9 January 1979, pp 7.

Robert standing in front of Ban Hock Hin at 131 Beach Road. Behind him, workers were preparing motorcycles for delivery to the Traffic Police. Circa 1973.

Honda CBX 750 motorcycles being prepared for delivery to Traffic Police. Ban Hock Hin won numerous bike and scooter delivery contracts from government bodies over the decades. Circa early 1990s.

Government contracts were not easy to secure or fulfil. Most had many requirements, and suppliers were expected to comply with them all. In the 1970s, one major distributor bid for and won a major military contract to supply about 250 units of recce bikes. Every bike had to be spray painted and retrofitted with special mounting for military equipment. The headlamps also needed to be modified for military use. There was a great deal of detailed work and documentation. After one contract, the major distributor decided it would be better to let dealers like Ban Hock Hin handle government contracts because of the huge amount of extra work involved.

One military contract, in particular, illustrated the intensity of effort required. In 1998, Ban Hock Hin won a military tender to supply reconnaissance bikes. However, these bikes had numerous specifications that no manufacturer met. Richard took a Yamaha bike closest in make and engine capacity, stripped it of its body parts, and rebuilt the bike according to the tender specifications. This sample bike was delivered to the military which then subjected the bike to harsh testing. They loaded the bike with 40kg worth of weight, rode it up a 40-degree slope, and let the bike tumble down the hill to see if it could withstand the abuse and keep operating. They even airlifted the bike using a helicopter and dropped it. Ban Hock Hin's modified bike passed with flying colours, and the company secured the tender.

Ban Hock Hin has also designed and built many customised products for government agencies and businesses over the decades. Whenever someone needed to move things on wheels, Ban Hock Hin was able to customise a solution. This was one business that Ban Hock Hin excelled at and few others could compete in. Therefore, when Robert decided to end the retail and hire purchase business in 1995, Ban Hock Hin concentrated on bidding for government and corporate tenders. It was especially good at customising livery, accessories, and even modifications. Robert's knack for efficient organisation and management of the production process and Richard's technical expertise made a potent combination. The years of reconditioning old bikes for export had given them valuable experience and confidence in fulfilling large orders on tight timelines.

One of the agencies that Ban Hock Hin often works with is the Singapore Civil Defence Force (SCDF), which is continually on the lookout for new technologies and more effective methods of fighting fires and saving lives. In 1994, Ban Hock Hin supplied its first batch of customised Fire bikes – Honda CB400 motorcycles retrofitted to carry fire-fighting equipment – to the SCDF. It went on to supply many additional batches of customised firefighting and paramedic two-wheelers. It also designed motorised casualty transporters for its HazMat teams so they can evacuate casualties from hazardous sites more quickly and effortlessly. In the 2000s, Ban Hock Hin also supplied three-wheelers for SCDF's emergency response teams. The three-wheeled vehicles were more stable and thus were safer and easier to operate.

SCDF wasn't the only organisation to benefit from Ban Hock Hin's ingenuity in designing unique products on wheels. The company also designed and supplied special firefighting equipment trolleys for use in Singapore Prisons as well as motorised track trolleys for the Land Transport Authority to use in the MRT tunnels. It even supplied motorised trolleys to transport heavy documents and parcels in regular office environments.

Companies like SingPost, SembCorp Environment and logistics company Transnational Group also turned to Ban Hock Hin to design three-wheeled vehicles to help them raise their productivity and reduce costs. SingPost needed a way for postmen to transport more mail. SembCorp needed a solution to help its cleaners transport more refuse when it wasn't necessary to use the large dumpster trucks commonly associated with refuse disposal. Transnational needed their delivery riders to be able to carry more parcels. In these cases, Ban Hock Hin turned scooters into three-wheeled vehicles with extra-large customised boxes or bins built into the rear.

Physically disabled motorists also turned to Ban Hock Hin for help with their unique transport needs. For example, a client needed a cost-effective vehicle that could accommodate his wheelchair. Ban Hock Hin fitted a Gilera scooter with the moulded rear of a Suzuki Swift to create an eye-catching hybrid vehicle that he could use with his wheelchair. It came with a seat belt and a ramp as well as the ability to reverse. Although a vehicle like that cost about $20,000 – double the cost of a regular scooter – it was still far cheaper than a car.

Ban Hock Hin's move to a large site in 6, Defu Lane 4 in 1990 gave the business much needed room to expand its workshop and its operations. At the Defu site, Ban Hock Hin had space to work on the large numbers of corporate or government two-wheelers. It now has a dedicated customisation area, fibreglass workshop and spray-painting workshop.

Changing the Game

Supplying bikes to fleet owners got Robert thinking about how fleet owners maintained their machines, whether they ran their own workshops or whether they engaged vendors. He thought deeper into the troubles and inconveniences that fleet owners faced when operating their fleets, especially if they didn't have a large enough fleet to warrant setting up and maintaining their own workshop and vehicle rescue teams.

Having been in this trade for decades, he understood how some riders thought and what some of the common tricks were. Riders would sometimes sabotage their own bikes and call it a breakdown to get some respite from the drudgery of their day. It wasn't uncommon for workshops to find a dented spark plug head in a bike that had 'broken down'. Sometimes, the riders would conspire with workshops to file false reports or to inflate invoices, either to split the illicit gains or to justify a longer downtime for the bike. If the riders' personal bikes were of the same make and model as their company bikes, the tyres of the company bikes would mysteriously wear faster than normal. All these antics added to companies' financial and operational costs.

He knew that vehicle maintenance costs could be difficult to predict and to manage, especially if organisations outsourced their vehicle maintenance. He also knew the challenges of running a labour-intensive operation such as a vehicle workshop if they operated their own. Robert figured that if it wasn't easy running this kind of operation – and Ban Hock Hin was the trade expert – what more for fleet owners whose main functions weren't even in motorcycles.

Workshops also needed a reliable spare parts department or store to operate effectively. Yet, managing a spare parts store also came with its own set of challenges. It took consistent care and effort to ensure that items were properly stocked, organised, and stored so the right parts were available and easily located and retrieved when needed. Keeping accurate and up-to-date records of the stock items alone was no easy task. Missing items and stock discrepancies were common as were inaccurate or incomplete records. When the scale of operations increased, these problems – and their attendant costs – often multiplied.

Yet, every minute a vehicle was in the workshop for repairs was a minute it was not in service. This not only hindered organisations' operations, it also represented a form of cost as the equipment was not being used productively while its value continued to depreciate. Large fleet operators often had to keep spare motorcycles as backup in case any of the regular in-service vehicles broke down. Those spare motorcycles added to the cost of fleet maintenance and operation.

Robert thought deeply about the challenges that fleet owners faced and how he could solve them. If he were them, what solution would *he* want? Hence, he designed a service that would solve all the fleet owners' problems. This comprehensive package would include the vehicle, insurance, road tax, regular servicing, repairs, and parts. If vehicles broke down, the package would provide not only towing services but also a replacement bike so the fleet owner's business could carry on. In essence, fleet owners would only need to lease the bikes and have almost all their bike-related needs met. In Robert's words, "All they need to do is fill up the gas tank."

Fleet owners who already owned their own bikes or wished to do so would still need maintenance and repair services. The costs of such services also could fluctuate, which made budgeting and accounting more difficult. Slow and inefficient maintenance and repair could adversely affect operations. Robert thus devised the Comprehensive Maintenance Plan or CMP. This plan would include regular servicing, replacement of parts, towing of broken-down bikes, and a replacement bike while the broken-down bike was under repair – for a fixed monthly fee per bike. A fixed monthly fee would give a fleet owner absolute control over its fleet maintenance cost. To take it one step further, he added a component called the Collision Damage Waiver or CDW to take care of all accident repairs as well, even the excess that insurance required the insured to pay. In short, a fleet owner's cost projections and cost management would remain constant. A fleet owner would be responsible only for intentional damage or sabotage.

The problem was Robert didn't know how much these dream services would cost Ban Hock Hin to provide, and therefore, how much to charge clients. But he had an ace up his sleeve – he knew that his computer system could collect and analyse maintenance and breakdown information unlike any other in the market.

The computer system that Robert started building in the early 1980s and grown over the years. Robert had added more modules, including one for the workshop and the store. He called it the Integrated Business System (IBS). He had also switched from using IT vendors to hiring staff for an in-house IT department to continually improve and adapt the IBS to keep pace with changing business needs.

The workshop module collected servicing and repair data of every bike, the dates and times it checked in and out, the mileage at every visit, every part used, and every event in its maintenance and repair history. With this information, Robert could assess the maintenance costs of bikes used in every industry and for each company. He could see usage patterns and even spot rider mischief. With time and data, Robert could gather intel that no one in the industry had. The computer system he was building had no equal in the trade.

All Robert needed to do was to start offering leasing and CMP and start collecting data – he could adjust the fees later when he had more data on which to calculate prices. He said: "In business, it is a chicken and egg situation. If you cannot make a decision, you cannot start. So, I decided to just quote a figure to the customer and start collecting data. With more data, we can adjust our prices."

The first customer to take up this unique service was Bax Global, an American international shipping company. Bax Global had approached Ban Hock Hin around 1993 to buy 10 motorcycles. Robert convinced the company to give leasing a try, and he offered a very low monthly fee of around $120/month, inclusive of the vehicle, insurance, and full maintenance and vehicle rescue package. Because the Piaggio Sfera was considered an 'old' model by then – the Skipper was already on the market, and the Hexagon was going to be launched soon – Robert offered the Sfera to Bax Global. This allowed Robert to get rid of old Sfera stock, which was another business win.

With leasing, Bax Global needed to start paying only the monthly fee of $120, which, for 10 bikes, amounted to only $1,200 per month. If it bought the bikes at $4,000 each, it would have to spend $40,000 at a go. And all this was without calculating the branding and accessories that corporate bikes typically bore. From an accounting and financing perspective, leasing was a more attractive option. The big question was whether Ban Hock Hin could deliver on these lofty promises. Bax Global took a chance and leased the 10 bikes it needed instead of buying them as planned.

A few years later, the next large contract came through another logistics company – Transnational Supply Chain Logistics. It leased 60 to 80 bikes. They could easily add and reduce the number of bikes as and when they got new contracts or ended old ones.

The success of a new product or service is also dependent on some amount of luck and timing. Toward the latter half of the 1990s, food delivery services were becoming popular. Many of these companies were small-medium enterprises for whom a one-stop service like the ones Ban Hock Hin provided were particularly attractive.

The Canadian Pizza Group became the next group of leasing clients. They took about 40 bikes. Other food delivery businesses soon followed suit, and Robert's new leasing and CMP services grew more and more popular.

Robert used these initial contracts to learn the ins and outs of providing leasing services and to collect precious data. He used the lessons to finetune his operations and his IBS computer system. He learned the finer points of building and managing the team needed to produce consistent results and deliver on the promises to clients.

He made sure to ingrain the values of accountability and integrity into the company culture. These qualities were not only part of Robert's personal credo but also essential in building successful long-term business relationships. And the leasing and CMP services he designed were inherently long-term businesses. Regardless of the manpower, human resource or operational challenges that Robert faced, one thing was non-negotiable – that of delivering on the promises made to the clients. For example, no matter what it took, he ensured that a motorcycle rescue team was at the site of a client's vehicle breakdown within the hour with a replacement bike ready, as promised.

Years later, Robert's son, Rex, would also demonstrate similar dedication to fulfilling promises. During times when the company suffered labour shortages – whether from staff taking sick leave or during unusually busy periods – Rex would work 18 to 20 hours each day to ensure deadlines big and small were met.

In essence, Robert brought together three key assets – his knowledge of fleet owners' needs, his problem-solving skills, and his computer system – to create new services and new market opportunities. In doing so, he changed the market and created a new way forward for Ban Hock Hin.

2000-2019: Riding to New Heights

Taking Pole Position

The new millennium started with a bang for Ban Hock Hin. It managed to secure a maintenance contract for one of the largest fleet owners on the island – Singapore Post Ltd (SingPost). Blue-clad postmen zipping about on white scooters delivering the country's mail was a common sight, and that's because Singapore's postal carrier had nearly 1,000 two-wheelers on the road.

Robert convinced the director in charge at the time, Lim Kay Hwan, to outsource the huge fleet's maintenance to Ban Hock Hin. It was a big gamble for both SingPost and Ban Hock Hin. Up until that point, SingPost had operated their own workshops and managed their own maintenance. But as Robert had already ascertained, operating a workshop was a costly and time-consuming operation, especially as vehicle repairs were only an auxiliary function of the postal services company. Outsourcing that troublesome function to the experts seemed the most logical course of action. Robert remembers Mr Lim telling him: "You better make sure you do it properly, Robert; my head is on the chopping block!"

Undertaking that huge contract was a big challenge for Robert and his team. He sat down with his IT, admin and workshop teams to hash out the most effective way to take over the maintenance schedule smoothly. The company's reputation – and the client's operations – were at stake. To accommodate such a large fleet, numerous changes had to be made to the way the teams worked. And yet, despite the challenges to his own operations, Robert also considered all the ways he could organise the maintenance with minimal disruption and maximum convenience to SingPost.

Instead of having SingPost deliver their bikes to Ban Hock Hin's Defu Lane workshop, Robert outfitted several trucks with a mechanic's tools and spare parts, turning them into mobile workshops. These mobile workshops would then carry out maintenance and simple repairs at the bases where SingPost's bikes were parked. When more complex repairs were needed, the trucks would tow the bikes back to Ban Hock Hin's workshop. The condition and mileage of every bike at every servicing, the parts used, and any notable observations would be recorded by the mechanic. The data would be recorded into the IBS. The IBS was tweaked to capture the additional information needed to produce customised reports for SingPost. Admin staff were reshuffled and retrained.

The data the team collected was priceless. It gave the company and its client new and detailed insights into the use and wear of the vehicles. When issues came up, such as whether damage was caused by normal or abnormal use, the maintenance history of the bike became indispensable to the investigation and assessment. It also gave SingPost assurance that its fleet was being cared for methodically and meticulously. SingPost was even able to increase its cost savings.

Ban Hock Hin's success at maintaining the health of the SingPost fleet, reducing the number of vehicle breakdowns, increasing the speed of response to breakdown vehicles, and reducing the amount of repair time for each vehicle meant that SingPost could shrink the number of replacement scooters it kept as backup. Because SingPost needed to maintain its corporate image, its postmen had to use SingPost scooters for mail delivery. This meant that the company needed to keep a fleet of scooters bearing the appropriate livery on standby. When Ban Hock Hin first took over the contract, there were 54 replacements scooters. Within six months, that figure was whittled down to 30. By the end of the first year, SingPost found it needed to keep only 10 scooters. When SingPost management wanted to know if the replacement fleet could be further reduced, Robert printed the usage report for the replacement fleet, which showed the number of replacement scooters used each day. With this data, SingPost management could make the decision to keep 10 replacement scooters with confidence.

Ban Hock Hin went on to complete the contract successfully and was able to easily win the subsequent maintenance contracts. SingPost's confidence in Ban Hock Hin also led to other business opportunities. When the mail delivery company wanted to increase its productivity, Ban Hock Hin proposed that it consider using a modified three-wheeler.

Ban Hock Hin's ability to use data to back up its claims and decisions helped to safeguard as well as build its sterling reputation for integrity. Shady practices were – and are – quite the norm in the vehicle workshop industry. Customers often have a hard time knowing whether they are being dealt with honestly and fairly. Robert set out to ensure that Ban Hock Hin's integrity was beyond reproach. Integrity, accountability and reliability are essential when dealing with government and corporate clients. Robert understood that longevity and success in this business depended on this reputation.

When things run smoothly, however, it is often easy to forget the principles and effort that make that success possible. Some motorcycle dealers have attempted to duplicate Ban Hock Hin's leasing and CMP products. They took Ban Hock Hin's pricing and undercut it by 10 to 20 per cent, thinking that this would be an easy strategy to enter the corporate market. Some clients have been swayed by the savings the newcomers offered. Most times, the results were less than satisfactory.

Many of those clients return to Ban Hock Hin after trying out other service providers for a term or two. They often bring tales of underhanded tactics, repair short cuts, and failed promises. For example, one competitor used cable ties to hold together worn parts instead of replacing them. That workshop also poked holes into clogged air filters instead of replacing them. Such tactics often cause additional damage to the machines.

Ban Hock Hin continued to build on its reputation and success from the turn of the millennium. It secured leasing and maintenance contracts from numerous large fleet owners and well-known brands such as McDonald's and KFC. The spectacular rise of food delivery services helped fuel the growth of Ban Hock Hin's leasing products. Because leasing arrangements are based on relatively short-term contracts of one or two years, companies can scale the size of their fleet more closely to actual demand. As they pay only a monthly, three-figure leasing fee, they can also do this cost effectively without investing heavily in buying new bikes that cost thousands of dollars each. This made for easy accounting and budgeting as well as cost control. There was no downside for the customer.

Ban Hock Hin also provided even shorter-term lease, on a daily, weekly or monthly basis. This proved invaluable to organisations, especially those involved in special events.

For example, when U.S. President Donald Trump and North Korean leader Kim Jong-un decided to meet in Singapore, the republic's security agencies had to increase the number of officers they deployed, including those on two-wheelers. Unfortunately, they didn't have enough in their existing fleet. Ban Hock Hin was able to supply 30 to 50 units of motorcycles to the traffic and auxiliary police to meet their temporary demand. These leased/rental bikes even came with full livery. During other large-scale events, such as the annual Formula One races, the security agencies also turned to Ban Hock Hin to meet their short-term increased need for vehicles.

Ban Hock Hin became the go-to problem solver for many organisations. It was often able to help clients in ways that few industry players could. Furthermore, the successful leasing programme also brought Ban Hock Hin even greater influence in the industry. Under this arrangement, Ban Hock Hin decided the brand and model of bikes to be leased. Because Ban Hock Hin served fleet owners, it dealt in large numbers of bikes, and its large orders often gave it more bargaining power and influence with suppliers. Robert's bold move to change the focus of the business from sales to service had once again showed his vision and foresight.

Passing the Torch

In 2009, when Robert turned 70, he turned the company over to his youngest son, Soon Cheong – or Rex – to run. Rex was 30 years old, the same age Robert was when he took over Ban Hock Hin from San Chwee. Robert stayed on as chairman of the board, but he left the operations to his youngest son to manage.

Rex has inherited Robert's drive to continually find better ways to do things; he also came armed with skill and knowledge in both the mechanical and digital fields. In the first decade of his stewardship, Rex upgraded the IBS to a Windows-based operating system, automated routine admin tasks, reorganised the workshop and streamlined operations.

In the past, mechanics used paper forms to record each repair job's data and to draw spare parts. Rex made workshop operations paperless by having the mechanics use smart tablets to perform these functions instead. They can also request for parts from the parts catalogues and prepare quotations directly from the tablet. This has improved the accuracy of the data collected and reduced the number of steps needed for each process. It also gives the team leaders real-time information about the status of all repair jobs and the workshop's workload so they can manage operations more effectively.

Although some of the older staff were initially a little afraid of the new technology and unfamiliar ways of doing their work, Rex helped ease them in by training them and assigning mentors to support them. Once they got used to the new technology, there was no looking back. The mechanics I spoke to not only told me how the smart tablets made their jobs easier, they also talked about how proud they were of being able to learn and use something so new and modern.

But Rex didn't stop at finding and implementing better ways of doing things on his own; he made continual improvement part of the company culture. Staff are encouraged to submit ideas for improvements, and if those suggestions are not adopted, the management will take pains to explain the reasons. He built in new procedures – even requirements – for every department to regularly submit ideas for improvement and feedback for other departments. These initiatives have resulted in a constant stream of ideas and, more importantly, improvements to how things are done. For example, the IT department alone makes an average of 30 changes to the IBS each month.

Mechanics use smart tablets to prepare and capture all the paperwork needed in the course of their servicing and repair duties.

His engineering background – Rex was trained as an aerospace engineer – meant he was able to devise new and better ways of meeting clients' special transport needs. He was also able to provide leadership and expert insights to his technical team and troubleshoot – and solve – mechanical problems even more effectively.

To better understand his clients, Rex took up motorcycle riding and racing soon after he started working at Ban Hock Hin. He went to riding schools to hone his skills and grew to be quite a racing enthusiast who was able to accomplish respectable lap times on the racetrack. He became a US-certified riding coach and helped his trainees ride safer even while going faster.

Like Robert, Rex also understood that the lifeblood of a business was its people, and he took pains to attract and retain talent. He drew up career roadmaps across the organisation, fine-tuned or adopted human resource policies, and introduced people development programmes such as the Leadership Management System (LMS). In 2018 and 2019, company invested some $180,000 on leadership training for its staff.

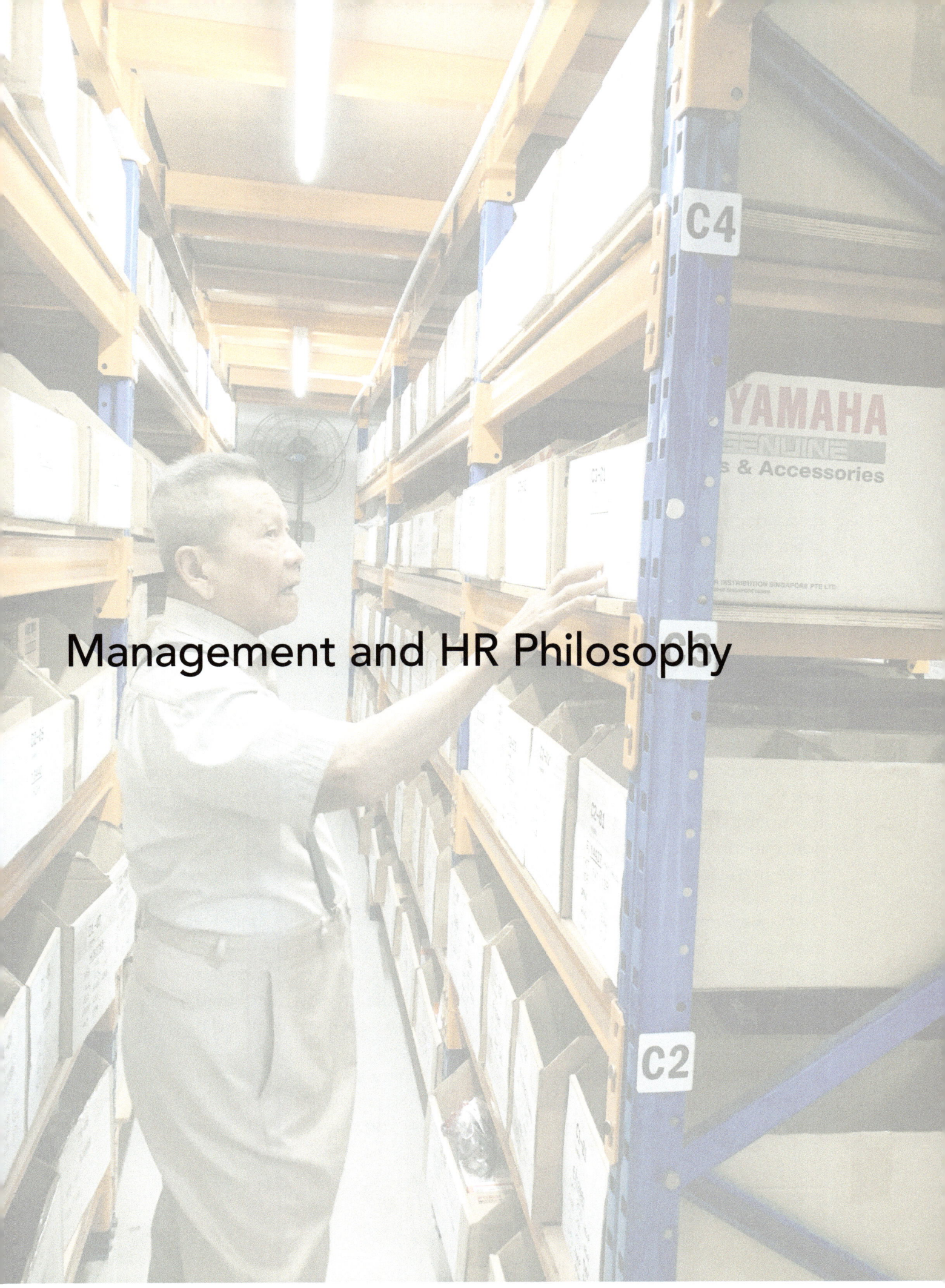

Management and HR Philosophy

Robert believes that a critical factor in business success is sound and far-sighted management. He said: "Sales and marketing are important, but without proper management, a business cannot survive. But management alone is not enough; you need sales and marketing to bring in revenue. In business, you need both."

Robert's management skills weren't confined to Ban Hock Hin alone. An entrepreneur at heart, Robert has started or invested in many other businesses over the years. He's helped shepherd many of them to success.

Auto Machinery Supply Pte Ltd (AMS) started as a small spare parts company with a value of $60,000 in 1981. Robert was initially an investor, but he didn't involve himself with the business' daily operations except on rare occasions.

For example, he pushed for the computerisation of the business in the 1990s after he saw the benefits that a computerised stock system yielded for Ban Hock Hin. However, even then, he faced some pushback, although no one was bold enough to object to his face.

But in the early 2010s, AMS ran into problems. Each year, the spare parts company had to conduct a stock take, after which the accounts could be finalised and closed. Most years, the stock take results were unsatisfactory with high stock variance. This meant that a high percentage of the type, quantity and location of parts did not match the records. The shareholders just bore with the poor results as long as the business continued to make money.

However, one year, the staff took four to six months to conduct the stock take, and even so, struggled to complete it. Hence, the accounts were in danger of not being settled in time for the closing of the financial year. Even worse, the team had hired temporary staff to carry out the stock take. Robert was furious because the full-time staff were not involved in this important exercise – it reflected a lack of responsibility and accountability. He also saw the mess that the company was in – boxes of spare parts littered the shop floor and the stock items were chaotically strewn about. With some 8,000 types of items in stock – not counting the quantities held for each item – it looked near impossible to find anything in the mess. He was enraged at the lack of care he saw in the situation.

He pushed for the shareholders to withhold the year-end bonus until the stock taking exercise was completed. He initially faced fierce objections, but he argued that if the problems – both the stock take exercise and the lack of proper management – were not resolved, this company should be shut down. It would be a matter of time before it failed anyway. The logic was sound, and the shareholders agreed to withhold bonuses.

Robert then became personally involved in cleaning up the business. He brought in an experienced spare parts executive to support AMS through the clean-up and to report regularly to Robert. He set about to methodically sort out the problems at AMS.

First, he set up a proper storage and location system – shelves were named and labelled. Boxes were standardised so things would appear uniform and neat. They were also labelled so staff could easily identify the items each was supposed to hold. Every item had to be properly labelled, and its location had to be recorded into the computer database. Parts were painstakingly sorted and organised. Robert then found that the stock variance that year was nearly $50,000 – a huge amount. At these levels of variance, it would be difficult to detect or prevent pilferage. Lack of proper management led to multiple losses for a business and its stakeholders.

Reorganising AMS took time and a great deal of effort, but Robert persisted, and a year later, AMS was transformed.

The next year, the team only needed three days to complete the stock taking exercise. Only a single item was found out of place or missing. Robert upped the ante – he told the staff that if they could achieve 100 per cent accuracy, the entire team would enjoy a free overseas trip. The team has managed to achieve 100 per cent accuracy several years in a row. This kind of stock accuracy is nearly unheard of in the industry. It also brought multiple benefits.

In the past, the stock that AMS held was valued at about $1.2 million. With the improved system, it now only needs to hold $400,000 in stock. This translated to savings in terms of storage cost, interest cost and the 'freshness' of the stock. In other words, stock levels were optimal, stock turnover was health, and stagnant stock was minimal.

The staff morale now is also riding high. They feel proud to have been able to achieve such a feat. The neat and airy environment they now work in is also far more pleasant than the chaotic one from before. Their daily tasks were also easier to carry out because they could quickly find the items customers wanted. They could also deal with customers with confidence. Each year, they look forward to achieving 100 per cent stock accuracy and going on their incentive trip.

The staff have taken on the mindset of continuous improvement. During a recent visit to AMS, the staff proudly rattled off all the improvements they were implementing or have implemented in the business.

AMS now operates two branches and holds several properties. The business is now worth millions.

Robert inspects AMS premises. Shelves and boxes are clearly labelled.

At AMS, boxes and shelves are lined up neatly and walkways are kept clear. Neat and systematic organisation makes it easy for staff to locate parts for customers.

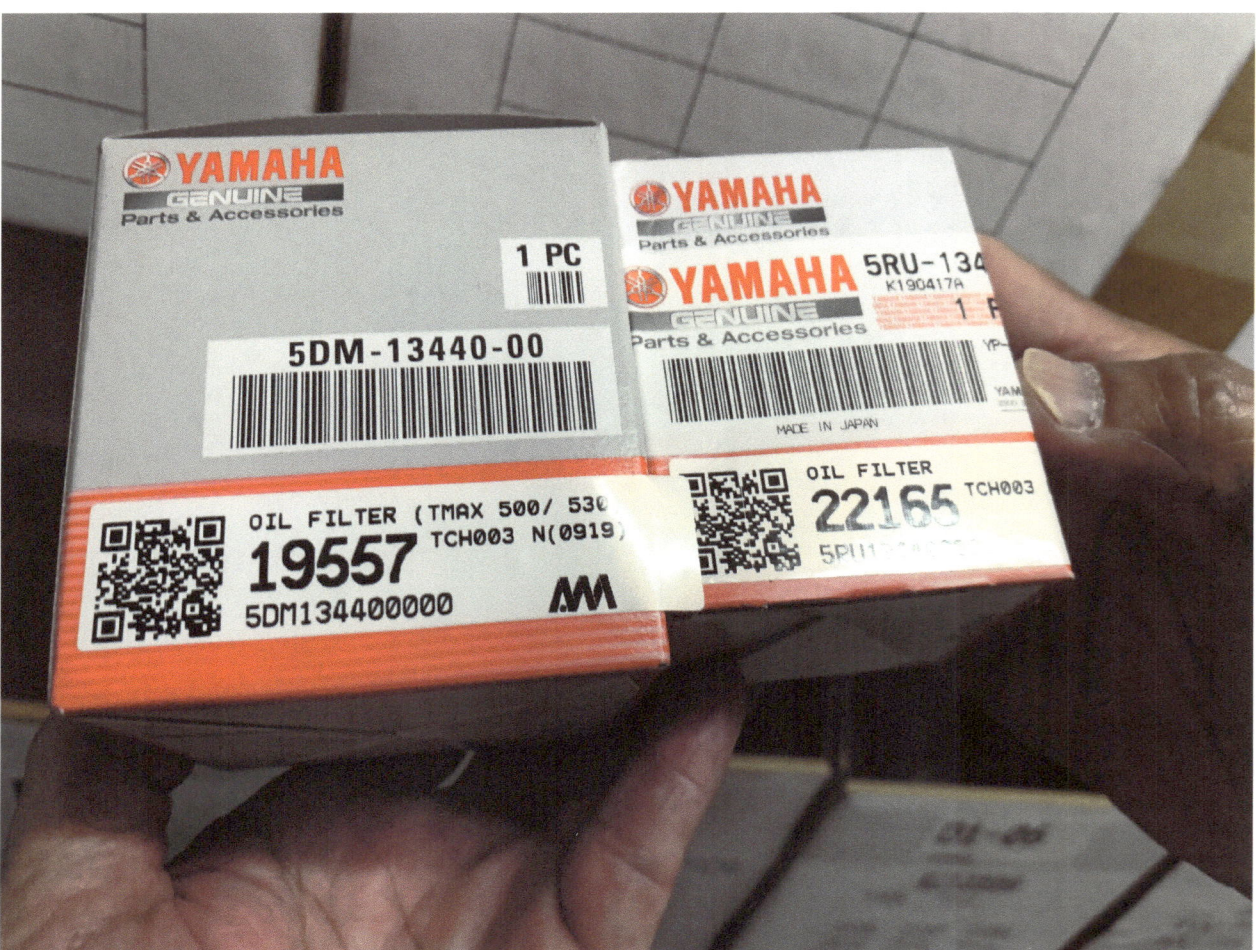

AMS has started using QR codes to label parts, an example of the spirit of continual improvement that the motivated staff members have embraced.

In addition to sound management, Robert also believes that another critical factor in business success is its people. The right talent and mindset make all the difference, especially for a business that provides services and not just sell products.

As a result, when Ban Hock Hin switched to providing leasing and CMP, Robert intensified his support for his people. He invested a lot of time to motivate, engage and encourage his team, further honing his already formidable skills of persuasion and inspiration. It was common to see an angry or downhearted employee emerge with smiles and renewed vigour after a long one-on-one talk with Robert.

He often took his staff out to meals or provided lunches and dinners during meetings or busy periods. He got to know every person very well and was able to identify – and bring out – the best in each.

For example, there was a staff member whose only experience before joining Ban Hock Hin was on the factory floor as a production worker. She had little education and even fewer management skills. Under Robert's tutelage and encouragement, she eventually came to manage the operations of the leasing department and was able to handle clients and solve problems. In another example, a young man joined Ban Hock Hin's workshop team as an apprentice barely out of his teens. Robert nurtured him and gave him opportunities to develop his skills. That young man eventually became the chief mechanic and manager overseeing the team in charge of special projects, which required creativity, ingenuity and project management abilities to fulfil clients' unique requirements.

Robert also knew that each employee was a person first. Few could compartmentalise their personal lives and leave their personal troubles at the company's gates, regardless of the ideals of professionalism. Hence, Robert would go the extra mile in helping his people out in their personal or financial situations whenever he could, often dipping into his personal time and finances to do so. He said: "When you care for your staff, your staff will be more prepared to put in their effort for you."

Robert's kindness to his staff was not always reciprocated, however. There have been too many instances where staff would approach him with heart-breaking stories of family tragedy and need, only to disappear once they secured a loan from Robert. Some employees that Robert mentored and nurtured would turn on him. One year, his workshop chief and mechanics bet heavily on a big sporting event and almost everyone came away with heavy losses. Those losses made some desperate – desperate enough to distract them from their work or worse, steal from the company.

But Robert never let these disappointments harden him toward his people in general – he continued to believe in the best of them, and he continued to extend loans and kindness to members of his team. That didn't mean that Robert was a pushover, though. His incendiary temper was legendary. Where his support and encouragement could be lavish, his disapproval and anger could be equally searing. I remember sitting in a meeting once when Robert was expressing his intense displeasure at something (or someone) to a degree where I was terrified that he was going to have a heart attack. All his staff feared and respected him in equal measure.

When the company struggled to turn in good profits during some lean years and couldn't afford to pay year-end bonuses, Robert paid every employee at least one-month worth of bonus out of his own pocket. He said: "Our people need the extra money to celebrate the new year. Even if the company can't pay, I must pay." With some 80 members of staff then, Robert spent hundreds of thousands of dollars to take care of his team.

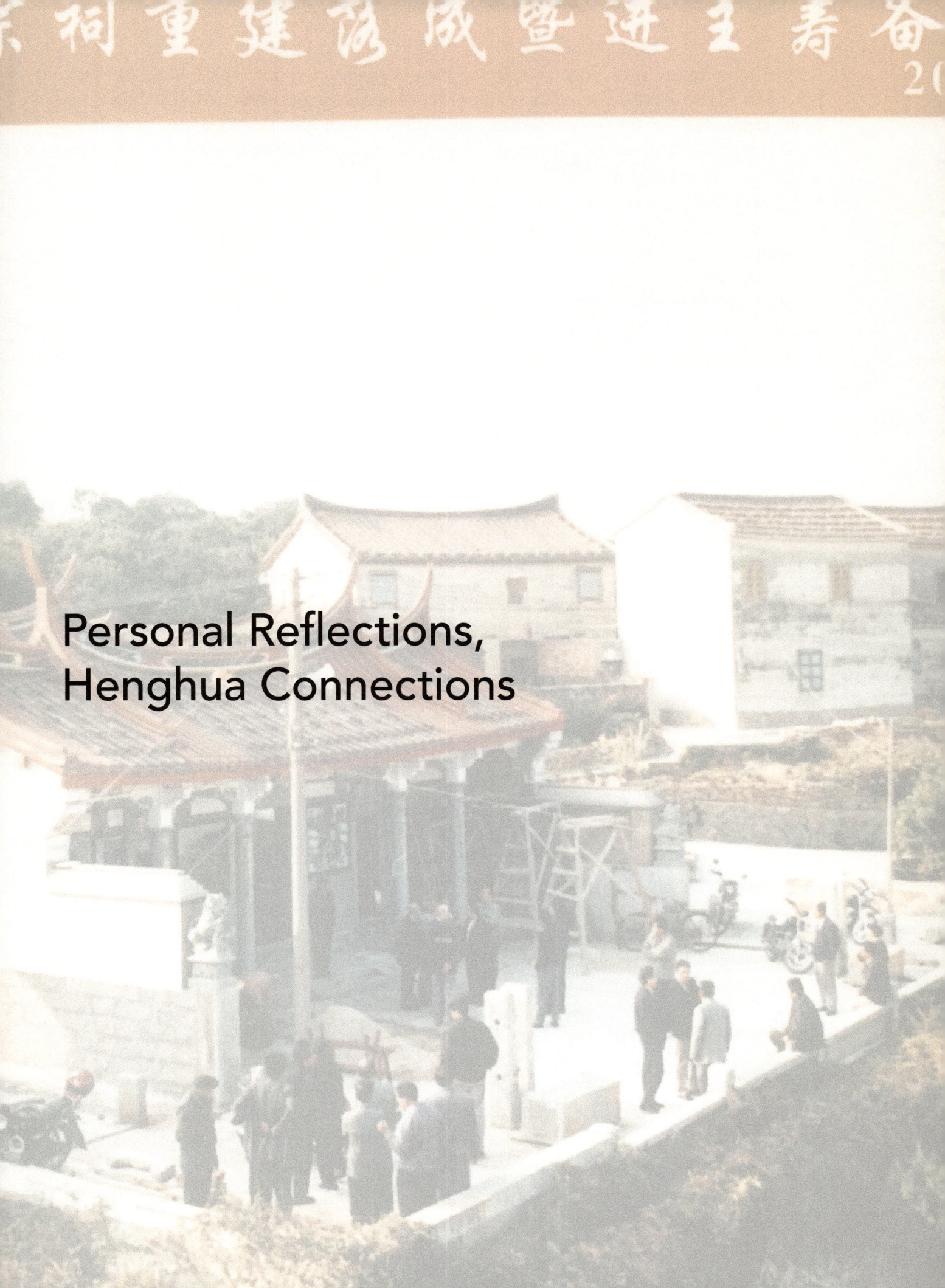

Personal Reflections,
Henghua Connections

Robert remembers spending time during his early years with his maternal aunt, whom he called *Ma Yee*. Where Kim Lian had been left largely uneducated, *Ma Yee* had been highly educated in the Chinese classics and liked to talk about Chinese culture and values such as the filial duties of a Chinese son. She'd also tell stories of Chinese history and lore. These tales that were full of ethics and Confucius values became seeds in Robert's young mind, and later, they would be the moral beacons that guided his thinking.

It might also have been *Ma Yee*'s lessons that embedded a love for Chinese culture and language in Robert, and in retirement, he discovered a love for Chinese period dramas that brought those tales and lore to life. He was especially fond of those about Chinese classics such as Three Kingdoms or about the various emperors and dynasties. The political intrigue and manoeuvrings appealed to his intellect, and his Mandarin skills, especially in Chinese proverbs and idioms, improved as a result.

During his semi-retirement in the early 1990s, Robert found himself the opportunity to visit his ancestral village in China. He had gone to Los Angeles with his wife Alice to visit Sam Gwee, the popiah king, who was spending time there because one of his children was studying in the city. Robert was also in the U.S. because his eldest son, Eng Joo (Juice), was attending a military school in Florida. During Robert's visit, Sam asked if Robert was interested in visiting China with him as Sam was planning to visit his ancestral village. Sam was Hock Chia, which is a dialect group found in Fujian Province. His ancestral village was therefore in Fujian province and close to Robert's ancestral village Dong Ao. In fact, Dong Ao, despite being populated by Henghua people, was administered by the Hock Chia prefecture.

At the time of Sam's suggestion to see China, it was not long after the Tiananmen Square incident in 1989, and relations between China and US had cooled considerably as a result. But Sam had good connections at the Chinese consulate, and he took Robert and Alice to get their visas. Sam then arranged for them to fly direct to Fuzhou, the capital of China's Fujian Province. It was Robert and Alice's first trip to China.

From the airport, Robert and Alice went with Sam to his ancestral village. Sam's brother-in-law drove. They then checked into the state dormitory/hostel as there were no real hotels yet. A Chinese official came by to see them before lunch, and Robert told him that he was interested in visiting Dong Ao. The official wanted to know who Robert was interested in at that village. All Robert had was his grandfather's nickname – Kow Sai – and the name of the village, Dong Ao (Dang Ou in Henghua).

He knew the village name only because San Chwee had set up an association for villagers from Dong Ao who had migrated to Singapore to work. This was about the time Robert was 10 years old, around 1949, when San Chwee was writing back to Dong Ao for labourers he could rely on to build his carriage tricycle. The association was a simple set-up – a hall where members could gather, rest, and, for those who had no money for rent, stay. Robert remembers visiting the Dang Oh association or *Dang Oh Hiu Li Guan* with San Chwee. It was a dim place with no electricity. Trishaw riders in blue pants would be eating, resting, or chatting quietly there. San Chwee would talk with each of them in turn, and for those who needed it, he'd give advice or money.

Now that Robert was in China, he wasn't sure if a place and a nickname would lead to much. Nor had he an inkling as to how long he'd have to wait for some results. Having done all he could, Robert and his companions then went to lunch.

Incredibly, when Robert returned from lunch, two men were waiting for him – one of them was Tan Hua Di. He was the grandson of Kow Sai's brother and, thus, was of the same generation as Robert. He would've called San Swee uncle.

Hua Di arranged for Robert, Alice, Sam, and Sam's wife and brother-in-law to return with him and his son to Dong Ao by car. When they drove up to the village entrance, some 40 people lined the streets waiting to welcome them. In that short time, they had made a banner with the word "欢迎" or "Welcome". Earlier on, Sam had advised Robert to prepare red packets or angpows for the relatives. Robert handed over a thick red packet to Hua Di and asked him to share it with the family. Robert noticed the keen eyes of those present following the red packet intently.

The villagers took the Singaporeans on a tour of the village. Dong Ao was a coastal village, and most of its inhabitants were fishermen. Muddy flats instead of white sand bordered the ocean. The houses were made of cement with no windows, to protect their occupants from the chilly gusts of wind from the ocean in winter. Kow Sai's old home still stood. It was a small, wooden structure with no plumbing or sanitation. The call of nature had to be answered in holes in the ground. Robert also got to visit his ancestor's tomb, and he was pleased to see that its *fengshui*, or its relation to the natural elements, was very good. The tomb sat on a hill facing the ocean, which is considered a prime location in Chinese geomancy.

Robert also visited the village's ancestral hall where ancestral tablets and family registers were housed. Traditionally, all Chinese families had a register to keep track of lineage and hierarchy of its members. Many Chinese names include a clan or family name, also known as a surname, and given names often comprising two characters. Many families also use generation names, which means using the same character for all members of the same generation as one of the two characters in the given names. The families are also likely to have a generation poem which spells out the sequence of generation names in a poetic format. Interestingly, neither Kow Sai nor San Chwee chose to use generation names for their children.

Part of the village tour included a generous snack. A very elderly woman filled a huge wok or *kwali* – which looked to be older than the cook – with water and poached numerous eggs for the guests. Each of the five Singaporeans was given four poached eggs, which was considered a feast by village standards. Unfortunately, only Alice was able to choke down one egg. The other Singaporeans couldn't stomach the idea of eating the eggs because of the condition of the *kwali* that they had been cooked in.

Before Robert and his company left the village, Robert pledged nearly S$100,000 to expand the village school and to build a playground. He dedicated the school extension to his father and called it "San Chwee Lau" (Hokkien) or *"Shan Shui Lou"* (Mandarin). He later donated additional sums of money at the villagers' request to help renovate the ancestral hall.

东澳村陈氏宗祠重建落成暨进主筹备会 2004.1.8

Photo of the Dong Ao ancestral hall as it was undergoing renovations. Robert had donated funds to support the renovation.

More than a decade later, Robert took his youngest son, Soon Cheong, and his family, as well as a few relatives and friends to visit Dong Ao again.

In His Words

Robert had some pet phrases to sum up his approach on various topics. Here is a small selection.

To succeed in a goal, Robert believed one needed three qualities: 信心 (xin xing)、决心 (jue xing)、耐心 (nai xing) – confidence in oneself, the determination to achieve one's goals, and the patience to wait for the results. Robert himself was a living example of this approach, especially when he set out to achieve outcomes that most others would consider too difficult or even impossible. These challenges included the time he introduced the use of computers in Ban Hock Hin, when he had to fulfil a 2,000-bike order, and when he rolled out the leasing and comprehensive maintenance programmes.

In leadership and management, he subscribes to the Chinese philosophy "以德服人"(yi de fu ren), meaning to gain submission, compliance or respect by treating others with virtue.

He is also keenly aware that long-term relationship building, especially in business, is dependent on mutual benefits. Hence, in all his business dealings, he aims for a win-win solution or arrangement.

His philosophy on investment of any kind: "Short-term pain is a long-term gain; but short-term gain is a long-term pain." Those who have foresight are willing to put up with short-term pain. He has applied this approach to all aspects of his business – from establishing the SMCTA to computerisation to the introduction of the leasing and maintenance products.

Robert was a skilled communicator who understood the number one rule of communicating effectively – that of understanding his audience. He'd often say in Hokkien: "*Tu tio lang, dio gong lang uay; tu tio gui, dio gong gui uay!*" meaning "When you meet a person, speak like a person; when you meet a devil, speak like the devil!"

Robert believed in the power of learning and teaching through example. His favourite quote on this matter was: "*Tai kway kah gao*" meaning "Kill the chicken to warn the monkey." Many of us around Robert have felt like either the chicken or the monkey at some point. There have also been times when we're not sure which we've been.

Robert has a great fondness for alcohol in social situations because he finds that it helps people relax and interact better. His favourite tipple is Hennessy XO. He prefers brandy, which is 'warm', over whisky, which is 'cold'. He'll occasionally enjoy a gin and tonic without ice. Ice was anathema to Robert, unless it was ice cream; then it had to be vanilla. Dinners were incomplete without at least a bottle of something potent in accompaniment. His advice for fending off intoxication was to drink a large glass of water with every serving of hard alcohol. And to line one's stomach with food, preferably good and fatty fare. Like his father, Robert enjoyed stewed pork belly and roast pork. Unlike his father, Robert exercised religiously. At 80, Robert does a total of 400 arm curls with 10 lb dumbbells in each hand every morning. He spends an average of two hours a day exercising. He also goes to sauna and foot reflexology sessions regularly to support his health.

When it came to drinking, anyone who drank regularly with Robert would be familiar with this Chinese saying, "酒逢知己千杯少，话不投机半句多" (jiu feng zhi zi qian bei shao, hua bu tou ji ban ju duo) meaning "among bosom friends, a thousand glasses are too few; when two people talk at cross purposes, a single sentence is half too much". If you're drinking with him and he breaks out this phrase, you'll know that he's thoroughly enjoying your company. Usually. Unless you've been disagreeing with him.

Robert reserved the Hokkien saying, "*Gu kia mm paht hor*" meaning "the calf doesn't recognise the tiger", for the inexperienced, gullible or over-reaching who try to tangle with the experienced or cunning. This phrase was most often used on newcomers to Robert's drinking table. Especially those who try to outdrink him or disagree with him. Then calf, meet chicken.

When it comes to assessing people, Robert likes to say that there are three kinds of people: "Those who make things happen, those who watch things happen, and those who wonder what happened."

When it comes to his treatment of others, though, he is fond of saying: "宁愿他人负我，我不负他人" (ning yuan ta ren fu wo, wo bu fu ta ren), meaning I'd rather others do wrong unto me than for me to do wrong unto others.

In general, Robert is not religious. He practices ancestor worship during Qing Ming as a mark of respect to his father and grandfather, but otherwise, he has never cared much for letting others tell him what rules to live by. Whenever he's asked about religion, he'd jokingly say, "I believe in any god that helps me make money!"

Other phrases he often uses include:

"*Gua kah li gong*", meaning, "let me tell you". He often starts his sentences this way. All his closest friends and kin, especially his grandchildren, would snigger a little each time he starts a sentence with that phrase. Everyone knew a lecture was coming up!

The catchphrase most associated with Robert, unfortunately, is a naughty one. He peppers his speech quite liberally – and expressively – with "*kanina*". He'll use it when he's angry, when he's surprised, when he's annoyed, and even when he's happy or amused. Quite a few of his grandchildren's early words included this phrase, much to the comic exasperation of his children and their spouses. If you don't know what this Hokkien phrase means, you'll have to find someone to explain it to you.

"三生有幸" (san shen you xing [Mandarin] or sa seng yew heng [Hokkien]) meaning that one has the blessing of three lifetimes or is most fortunate. This is sometimes paired with the Hokkien phrase *"Zhor kong wu leng"* meaning one's ancestors are effective, implying that ancestors had blessed the person in question.

Robert surrounded by his children and grandchildren during the 2019 Chinese New Year celebrations. Back row, from left to right: Anita (daughter), Ryan (grandson), Eileen (daughter), Shan (grandson), Maitrii (son-in-law), Lily (granddaughter), Michelle (daughter-in-law), Stephanie (daughter-in-law), Soon Cheong (son). Front row, from left to right: Maggie (granddaughter), Alice (wife), Sophie (granddaughter), Robert, Juice (son).

Lightning Source UK Ltd.
Milton Keynes UK
UKHW050613241119
354089UK00003B/15/P